INCLUSIVE JUDAISM

of related interest

People of the Book
An Interfaith Dialogue about How Jews, Christians and
Muslims Understand Their Sacred Scriptures
Dan Cohn-Sherbok, George D. Chryssides and Usama Hasan
Foreword by Marcus Braybrooke
ISBN 978 1 78592 104 9
eISBN 978 1 78450 366 6

Interfaith Worship and Prayer
We Must Pray Together
Edited by Christopher Lewis and Dan Cohn-Sherbok
Foreword by the Dalai Lama
ISBN 978 1 78592 120 9
eISBN 978 1 78450 385 7

The Role of Religion in Peacebuilding
Crossing the Boundaries of Prejudice and Distrust
Edited by Pauline Kollontai, Sue Yore and Sebastian Kim
ISBN 978 1 78592 336 4
eISBN 978 1 78450 657 5

Forgiveness in Practice
Edited by Stephen Hance
ISBN 978 1 84905 552 9
eISBN 978 0 85700 983 8

Learning to Live Well Together
Case Studies in Interfaith Diversity
Tom Wilson and Riaz Ravat
ISBN 978 1 78592 194 0
eISBN 978 1 78450 467 0

INCLUSIVE JUDAISM

THE CHANGING FACE
OF AN ANCIENT FAITH

JONATHAN ROMAIN AND
DAVID MITCHELL

FOREWORD BY MAUREEN LIPMAN

Jessica Kingsley Publishers
London and Philadelphia

First published in 2020
by Jessica Kingsley Publishers
73 Collier Street
London N1 9BE, UK
and
400 Market Street, Suite 400
Philadelphia, PA 19106, USA

www.jkp.com

Library of Congress Cataloging in Publication Data
A CIP catalog record for this book is available from the Library of Congress

British Library Cataloguing in Publication Data
A CIP catalogue record for this book is available from the British Library

ISBN 978 1 78592 544 3
eISBN 978 1 78450 939 2

Printed and bound in Great Britain

Contents

About the Authors

Jonathan Romain

Rabbi, writer and broadcaster, Jonathan Romain is minister of Maidenhead Synagogue. He writes for *The Times*, *The Guardian* and religious press, and is heard on the BBC. His books include *The Jews of England* and *Faith and Practice: A Guide to Reform Judaism Today*. He received the MBE for his work nationally in helping mixed-faith couples, a theme covered in his book *Till Faith Us Do Part* (HarperCollins). He is chaplain to the Jewish Police Association, president of the Accord Coalition for inclusive education and a vice-chair of Dignity in Dying. For several years he was a judge for both The Times Preacher of the Year Award and the BBC's Frank Gillard Awards. He is a past chair of the Assembly of Reform Rabbis UK and is on the Council of St George's House at Windsor Castle. His previous book, *Confessions of a Rabbi* (Biteback), has had wide coverage in the media.

David Mitchell

Rabbi, educator and LGBT+ advocate, David Mitchell is a member of the rabbinic team at The West London Synagogue of British Jews, the flagship Reform synagogue. Ordained at Leo Baeck College in 2009, for the last few years he has been a member of their faculty, assisting rabbinic students with their vocational training. Currently, he is researching for a PhD in Bible and Gender as a continuation of his MA degrees in Jewish Education and Jewish Studies. He has spent the last decade championing various inclusion changes within the Assembly of Reform Rabbis UK, was the founding co-chair of KeshetUK, is a patron of Save the Congo as well as an active trustee of the Jewish Aids Trust. His first publication was *Terror, Trauma and Tragedy*, co-edited with Jonathan Romain.

Both authors were born into Orthodox Judaism and were initially brought up within it. However, they each later changed to Reform Judaism and are among its leading representatives.

The term 'Reform' has been used as a shortened reference to Reform Judaism, and also to cover similar groupings, particularly Liberal and Progressive synagogues, who are organisationally different, but share most of the same principles.

Foreword

Maureen Lipman

Rabbi David Mitchell tells me that this book came about, in part, because of a conversation he and I had after synagogue one Saturday. We were walking through West London Synagogue as he was explaining about a historic change in Reform Judaism's approach to inherited status. He told me that it concerned children with a Jewish father and a non-Jewish mother, a matter very close to my heart. I responded with more emotion that I had expected, asking: 'Why hasn't this been better publicised? You ought to get the word out there'.

Well, they did and I'm glad to be a muse as well as amusing. In this book, Rabbi David Mitchell and Rabbi Jonathan Romain have not shied away from that challenge. They have addressed all the significant progressive changes of the last five decades, no matter how radical. Written for every Jewish home, this book includes real stories by real people. Here is mine:

> I grew up in Hull, in the 1940s where there were no Reform synagogues. There were three synagogues catering for 2,500 people. There are now only 227 Jews in last year's City of Culture and one tiny Lubavitch *shul* with no permanent rabbi.

The 'posh' *shul* was on Osborne Street, the middle-class one on Linnaeus Street and the third, Park Street *shul*, where my father was life president. He personally kept it afloat. Maybe he loved being a big fish in a tiny pond. Park Street *shul* was the congregation everyone looked down upon because it was the poorest. It was made up of two houses knocked into one, often with a part-time rabbi and no upstairs – a fact of life which upset my mother because she couldn't sit in the balcony in a big hat and chatter to her friends. All three congregations were Orthodox and the men and women were separated. Everyone was supposed to walk to *shul*, but few did. Usually, you parked around the corner and walked the last hundred yards, puffing. As Jews moved further away from the city centre this became a common and largely acknowledged deceit.

As a youngster, if you asked challenging questions about the hypocrisy of driving to the synagogue, but being banned from Saturday rugby or ballroom dancing there were no answers, just the occasional clip around the ear. Those unanswered questions came back at me like a kipper and turned my elder brother away from religion for life.

I discovered Reform Judaism through my late husband, Jack Rosenthal. Rabbi Percy Goldberg, a Reform rabbi in Manchester had converted Jack's first wife. Whilst the marriage had not lasted, Jack's affection for Reform Judaism continued throughout his life. I met Jack in Manchester in 1970. Four years later, living in London, we joined West London Synagogue. Rabbi Goldberg came down to officiate at our wedding.

I loved being part of a service which I could under-stand. It was intellectually challenging, and we were moved by the choir. Yet, living in Muswell Hill, the synagogue over in Marble Arch was quite a distance away, so we didn't attend often, even though both children went to the *cheder* (religion school) on Sundays...if we could schlepp them out of their beds. It took until our kids were a bit older before we attended more regularly. We were always fascinated by, and intellectually involved in the sermons of Rabbi Hugo Gryn. They were in stark contrast to the interminable and bone-grindingly boring sermons of my childhood. During the car journeys home, the whole family would discuss Hugo's sermon.

Later, Hugo and his wife Jackie, became friends and I think he once saved me from something akin to a nervous breakdown. I was a young mum of small kids in 1978 and performing in a play by Martin Sherman about the false Messiah, Shabbetai Zevi, playing a solitary, silent follower who has Woody Allen-like diatribes to her God. During one show a man stood up in the tiny, hot theatre and shouted abuse at me, accusing me of blasphemy. Even though I managed to complete the performance I felt scared and somehow assaulted. Fortunately, unbeknownst to me, Hugo had been in the audience. He rang me the next day and invited me to lunch. I couldn't believe that I was going to have a meal with a rabbi. As soon as I arrived, Hugo immediately put me at ease, recommending both the beef and chicken on the menu and giving me the reassuring code that I could eat what I liked. That conversation helped me to process the need for separating the actor from the human being, and that I needed more help at home.

I realised then that I was in the right place in a Reform *shul*. When I attend more Orthodox services, or when I am working abroad, I love to absorb the warm familiarity of tradition, the strong male voices and the richness of the vernacular, but I'm an observer there. In a Reform service I'm a participant. In the end, I realise that you only get out of any faith what you put in. One aspect which really hit me between the eyes was *Shabbat*, especially when my husband's health began to fail. Friday nights became so important because *Shabbat* was about stopping time – to relish it. Jack loved inviting friends round and we all enjoyed the chat and the laughter. Ever since then, Friday night has been about family time, albeit in a progressive way. Often, I am in my dressing room at the theatre – a dresser will pop her head round the door and say; 'Don't forget it's Friday. Have you lit your candles?' This I would do away from the beady eyes of the fire officer. Nowadays, I am often alone in my Manchester flat opposite the Rovers Return. I light my candles and eat my Ryvita and slug some Sauvignon – and just think. The happiest sentence I can hear as a mother and grandmother is: 'Are we at yours for Friday night?'

Over the years we've seen quite a number of changes in Reform Judaism, not least around inclusion and empowerment by making Judaism more inclusive and accessible. It's been an experience to see and get to know women rabbis. Programmed as I am, it has been a 'journey' as they say, to get used to the light timbre of so many female voices. I do enjoy watching boys and girls marking their *bar* and *bat mitzvah* as equal young congregants. Clearly, our religion was created by Middle Eastern men and the patriarchy has been used to instruct and suppress women. Reform Judaism redresses this imbalance and Jack and I were proud to be in a congregation with equal opportunities.

And yet, after all those years of membership, and all those years of raising proudly Reform children, I wasn't allowed to have a baby blessing for either of my grandchildren inside my own synagogue. A suitable conversion for my daughter-in-law seemed to be mainly about money; shades of the compromise, or, dare I say, hypocrisy of my youth, I thought. Without this dilemma, I probably wouldn't have known about patrilineal and matrilineal status until it became a personal problem. Due to an outdated policy of matrilineal descent we could not celebrate a blessing of the newest generation in the very sanctuary where we had been married and my son had marked his *bar mitzvah*.

Fortunately, The Liberal Jewish Synagogue opened their loving arms to us and, in time, both children were blessed by Rabbi Alexandra Wright in a beautiful, spiritual ceremony. Ultimately though, the Reform congregation at West London Synagogue was a place of nostalgia and familiarity for us; my partner Guido Castro has been a member for forty years, so we remained members.

However, it has to be noted that my grandchild's Jewish status was dictated by an archaic rule based on gender and patriarchy. It is meaningless to an antisemite whether a child has a Jewish mother or father; certainly, when Hitler came to power those categories did not save lives. Yet we pigeonhole ourselves and tie ourselves into knots about who can and cannot be an official member of our ancient and continuingly beleaguered people.

Every time I've seen a baby blessing since then I've thought to myself: 'Why not mine?' Furthermore, if we can have women rabbis, and women wearing prayer shawls, then why discriminate on this one issue? It was high time to change and that is why I am so pleased that Reform Judaism has finally come around to welcoming mixed-faith couples and embracing young Jews irrespective of the original faith or indeed the gender of their parents. After all, we need Jewish people now more than ever. The Jewish future is dependent upon us holding on to our own and accepting the whole of their Jewish identity and whomsoever they decide to love.

All of the welcome changes within this book are about securing a Jewish future I am full of admiration for those rabbis who have found new ways to maintain our ancient faith. For a more traditional Jewish family some of these developments might take a little while to get their head around. However, these are not theoretical challenges, they are real issues faced by ordinary Jewish families – maybe your own?

None of us has to look very far before identifying a loved one in a mixed-faith relationship, or who is a child of a Jewish father rather than a Jewish mother, or has 'come out' as LGBT+, or is a relative of such a member of our community; someone for whom the traditional approach to Judaism has failed to deliver a compassionate solution. It is precisely because each and every one of us in the Jewish community is affected, that we must embrace a more *inclusive* Judaism.

I myself don't eat *treif* (non-*kosher*), except for the odd crab sandwich in Ireland...I don't keep *kosher* but I rarely have milk after meat. I am aware that these dietary laws as well as the sexual laws and the necessity of circumcision were sensible and clever rules to avoid the perils of living in an unclean, sandy country in a burning hot climate.

I do what I can, living in a secular and clement land. I pray that is enough. I stand up as a ridiculously proud Jew and a proud Zionist. Our achievements are nothing short of dazzling. I hope this book will enlighten me and all its readers as to how we can progress, adapt to the times yet continue to remain so.

Maureen Lipman, CBE
Hon. doc. Tel Aviv, Salford,
Sheffield and Hull

Preface

Our object in writing this book has been to chronicle the remarkable changes that have occurred in Jewish life in recent decades – both the ways in which ordinary Jews live their lives and the responses that far-sighted rabbis have given so as to maintain Jewish values in new circumstances. They have attempted to do so without being fearful of crossing once-sacrosanct boundaries, and without being deflected by cries of protest by those who want to maintain the past exactly as it was. History will judge how successful this will prove, but there is no doubt that it is a challenge that cannot be avoided and that affects other faiths equally. The attempt to marry both tradition and change, and also to seek the good of both the community at large and the needs of individuals within it, are the most pressing religious tasks of our time.

Jonathan Romain and David Mitchell

Notes on the text

BCE refers to Before the Common Era
CE refers to the Common Era

Thanks are due to the many individuals in the book who have shared their stories. Some are their actual names, others are assumed names so as to protect their privacy.

1

Crisis? What Crisis?

The perilous state of British Jewry

For almost a century, British Jewry has been like a bath filled with water with the tap running, but the plug out. The water coming in was waves of new immigrants, the water going out was those departing from the community. It meant that the losses were compensated for by the gains, and the level remained more or less the same. Today, the situation has changed: the tap has been turned off, but the plug is still out, so there is a real danger of the bath emptying and British Jewry declining, rapidly.

While some readers will know that in the 2011 census, the size of British Jewry was estimated to be around 263,000, others will be shocked by it. Even if another 30,000 people are added to the total in order to make up for the Jews who were either wary of completing the census for historic reasons, or those born Jews who did not tick the box as they considered themselves to be secular, the figure amounts to less than 0.5% of the total population of the country. To put that in context, British Jewry is the size of Bolton or Brighton.

If this comes as a surprise, it is because British Jewry has always seemed to outsiders to be much more numerous than it is in reality. In fact, it can often feel much larger even to those within it. Popular images that come to mind are the Rothschilds, Marks & Spencer, Alan Sugar, Roman Abramovich, Simon Schama, Ed Miliband, Maureen Lipman, Howard Jacobson and Vanessa Feltz. The visibility of these and other high-profile Jews gives a totally misleading impression of the actual number of Jews. It shows that numbers are not essential in terms of impact, and it has often been said of the community that it 'punches above its weight'. However, where numbers do make a difference is in their effect on sustainability. The emptying bath may still be capable of making a splash, but its long-term future is much less certain.

To give a brief overview: although individual Jews had come to England as far back as Roman times, a settled community only arose when William the Conqueror brought Jews over from Normandy after 1066. Following a relatively peaceful century, conditions became increasingly hostile due to religious attacks by the Church and financial extortion by the Crown. The infamous massacre in York in 1190 is the most notorious of these events. All this culminated in Edward I expelling the Jews in 1290. They returned to England under Cromwell in 1656. This was partly because of the more sympathetic attitude of the Puritans, and partly because it was felt they would be economically helpful to the new Commonwealth. From then on there has been a continuous Jewish presence in the country (and meaning that it has been here longer than the Royal Family!).

The community grew slowly but remained small – some 30,000 by 1800 – until various groups arrived as a result of persecutions in their homeland. These included central European Jews from the 1830s to 1850s, a massive influx of Russian Jews in the 1880s to early 1900s, Jews from Germany, Austria and Czechoslovakia in the 1930s, those from Iran, Iraq and other Arab countries in the 1950s, South African Jews in the 1970s, as well as batches of Israelis (albeit for economic reasons), followed by French Jews since the 1980s.

The result was that the community increased dramatically to around 225,000 by 1900 and rose to around 400,000 by 1950. This, however, was its apex. From then onwards, numbers gradually decreased due to several different factors. One was emigration to Israel. The numbers were not vast – varying from decade to decade, but averaging at around 500 individuals per annum – but those involved were significant qualitatively, for they had a strong Jewish identity and would have been the most active within British Jewry had they remained. They also tended to be young singles or young families, so their departure not only reduced numbers, but lowered the birth-rate for the next generation. There is no doubt that Israel's gain was British Jewry's loss.

However, of far greater significance quantitatively was the decline brought about through assimilation and Jews falling out of the Jewish orbit. The reasons for their departure varied, but all had the same result of lowering the Jewish population dramatically. One group were those who deliberately shed their Jewish identity. For some of them, it was a matter of having experienced the effects of the Holocaust, be it directly or indirectly. Gretel – one of a considerable number of people who shared their stories for this book – spoke for many when she said:

> As a refugee from Germany who was lucky enough to get out on the Kindertransport, I have suffered greatly for being Jewish, and I see no reason why I should continue to do so. I have the chance to start a new life, so why should I leave myself open to the persecution I have endured up to this point?

Others who had experienced prejudice as a result of being Jewish left the Jewish community more for the sake of their children, so as to protect them from the possibility of any such re-occurrence. As Gerald explained:

> I can't escape my past, but I don't have to hand it on to my children. The best gift I can give them is being free from all the barriers and problems that our family has suffered for generations. I was picked on and bullied at school and I don't want them to be. If I can end it, I will be doing them a great service.

For other Jews, leaving the community was not so much a deliberate decision as a gradual process. They participated less and less in synagogue life or Jewish cultural associations. Over a period of time, they simply found that they had lost contact with all things Jewish. They no longer belonged to a synagogue, did not practise home ceremonies, and their friends were predominantly non-Jewish. They were like those travelling on an organised coach trip to a historic venue, who had simply wandered off on their own, not caring that they were missing the official tour or the return journey home. They were happy doing their own thing and oblivious to leaving the rest of the group.

Perhaps, even more numerically significant, were those who felt pushed into leaving the community because they had fallen in love with someone non-Jewish and 'married out'. Departing was not usually something they had intended, but the hostility with which their marriage was greeted meant that, as will be seen in more detail later (see Chapter 8), they no longer felt at home within the Jewish community, so they opted out of it. Of course, it meant that not only were they lost to British Jewry, but so were their children – a double blow.

The sexual revolution following the 1960s may have gradually liberated those who were gay, lesbian or transgender from the burden of hiding their identity, but acceptance from within the Jewish community, particularly the Orthodox, was hardly forthcoming. Those who at last felt free to be themselves in the wider world, still faced rejection within the Jewish one. As Brian put it:

If Judaism won't accept me, why should I accept Judaism?

Jesse typified those who not only felt hurt, but very angry:

What I find so difficult is not just the anti-gay sentiments that come my way, but the prejudice, injustice, insensitivity and lack of ethics underlying it all. Those are not my values and if Judaism is full of them, I don't belong there any more.

At the same time, many women, who held responsible positions in wider society, became increasingly resentful of their inability to be involved as active participants in either services or synagogue governance. Barbara spoke for many when she said:

> Why should I subject my capable daughters to invisibility
> and sexism? We wanted them to have every opportunity,
> but our synagogue felt like the absolute opposite, so
> we left.

There is also the God problem. For some Jews, God died in
the Holocaust: God's failure to intervene meant that God
no longer existed and may never have done. For others,
they were part of the general decline in the belief in God
within society at large. Science explained the origins of
life without a deity, so rituals began to lose their meaning
and prayer seemed to lack any power. As Harold put it:

> What was the point of being Jewish if I didn't sign up to
> Judaism any more?

Of course, there were Jews, as will be explored in Chapter
4, for whom lack of belief in a deity made no difference to
their Jewishness in other respects, and who were happy
to remain within the community. They labelled themselves
Jewish atheists or Jewish agnostics, and saw no conflict in
the different elements of those descriptions.

For the sake of completion, it should be noted that
there were other reasons for the declining size of British
Jewry, although not as statistically significant. One was
a small emigration of Jews to the United States during
the so-called 'brain drain' in the 1960s and 1970s. There
were also a number of Jews who converted to other faiths,
largely Christianity or Buddhism, but in both cases the
numbers were minuscule. Many of the latter retained
a Jewish identity, even earning themselves the generic
description of 'BuJew'.

It should also be added that the downward spiral in the population size was halted for the first time in 2016, when there was a slight growth reported. However, this was due to the high birth-rate among the ultra-Orthodox section of the community, with between six and ten children per family, sometimes more. But while they may have been boosting numbers through extra progeny, the factors mentioned above have not reduced the outflow of existing Jews – particularly those engaged with wider society and not leading isolated lives. This problem is still in force and will continue to denude the community.

There is another aspect. The decrease in size is not just a numerical issue, but also a reflection on the dour nature of British Jewry. Much of the losses it has sustained are because it has been inhospitable to its own members, unwilling to recognise the diversity among Jews today and reluctant to come to terms with the new types of Jewish identity. Jewish leaders have held on, dogmatically, to the image of all Jews being happily married. These idealised, happily married heterosexual couples will have at least one girl and one boy, will belong to a synagogue and will be keen to pass on their religious heritage. For too long, such community leaders have been blind to the fact that that this is far from the truth, for there are tens of thousands of British Jews who are divorced or non-believers or LGBT+ or discontent or living with non-Jewish partners.

If most Jews interact with society at large and have adopted contemporary liberal values, then Judaism has not only to speak their language, but it also has to remain in harmony with their values. This is not capitulation to modernity, but accommodation with it, wherever possible. Fairness, tolerance, justice and inclusivity are key secular values. They may not be part of the Ten Commandments, and may not have been emphasised in rabbis' sermons anywhere near as much as keeping *kosher* or observing the Sabbath, but nor are they alien to Judaism. If Jewish life is to hold the allegiance of modern Jews, those values need to be brought to the fore.

There will still be distinctions between Jewish life and the surrounding culture, but they will be because they are necessary, not because 'that is the way we have always done things'. There will still be some Jews who wish to isolate themselves from the general life around them, but most Jews feel at home in both worlds and do not want to have to make a choice between either of them.

The personal stories throughout this book have come from people whom we have encountered through our rabbinic work. Sometimes these people have been so keen for us to share their painful experiences, or their happy endings, or both, that they have written a full account, from which we have taken a key extract. Others have either dictated their words to us or asked us to represent their views by recalling our conversations with them. Where appropriate, especially in such a small Jewish community in the UK, we have changed names and identifiable details. Nevertheless, these are real people, and they are our people. They have real stories and real challenges which we need to hear and carefully consider. This book is also their book, for they want the message to get out that there is another way.

If British Jewry is to have a future, it has to become more user-friendly, and its rabbis have to learn to listen rather than growl when presented with new and challenging situations. We must adapt where appropriate, rather than automatically oppose. It is time to take down the barriers we have erected and instead put out the welcome signs.

2

The Immoral Bible

Let's be honest about the outdated attitudes in the Torah

In 1631, an edition of the Bible was printed with a serious mistake. The word 'not' was omitted in one of the Ten Commandments, with the text reading 'Thou shalt commit adultery'. Today, this can be regarded as an amusing typo, but at the time it was greeted with horror and seen both as blasphemy against God and endangering people's mortal souls by leading them into sin. The publisher was fined heavily, his licence to print books removed and he ended his days in debtors' prison.

However, there are many other passages in the Bible that were deemed perfectly laudable in the seventeenth century, but should be seen today as, at best, misguided and, at worst, immoral. There are those within the Jewish world who would regard with incomprehension the idea that any biblical verses could be less than perfect, taking the attitude that surely they are the word of God and therefore incontrovertible? The same would apply to many Christians who also treat the text as the living voice of God, whose truth never changes and whose commands must be obeyed. That view has, for instance, been crucial in the recent debates within the Church over the ordination of female priests and the sanctification of same-sex relationships.

In reality, though, it is only honest – and therefore, religious – to admit that among the many splendid and inspiring sections of the Bible, there are those that not only send shudders down our spine, but have also ruined the lives of innocent people. Such a perspective is predicated on viewing the Bible as *not* being the literal word of God, but the word of God as interpreted and relayed to others by individuals who were subject to the cultural limitations of their time. What seemed perfectly acceptable then – such as a system of slavery – is now regarded as abominable. Whereas some might consider it the height of arrogance to suggest that we know better than the religious greats of the past, surely it is the reverse: that it is the great success of religion when each generation tries to raise the moral bar to which it aspires. Key to this thinking is the concept of Progressive Revelation: that it was not a one-off moment of immutable truth given at Mount Sinai, but is an ongoing, ever-revealing process, with each age trying to understand the will of God for its own time; adapting as human knowledge and perceptions change.

The chained wife

One of the most pernicious aspects of the Bible is the fate of the chained wife. It relates to when a couple gets divorced. This is allowed in Judaism, which values marriage but does not insist that it become a lifelong prison if the relationship has broken down. In this respect, it is much more liberal than the New Testament, but unfortunately the wording of the process has caused hundreds of years of suffering for women. According to Deuteronomy 24:1–2, 'he writes her a bill of divorce, places it into her hand... and she is free to marry another man'. This apparently permissive act has the serious defect that the way it is phrased implies that it is initiated by the man. This led to subsequent Jewish tradition holding that divorce could *only* be initiated by the man. It meant that if he did not wish to divorce her, he could prevent it from happening.

The consent of the woman could sometimes be assumed by a rabbinic court, but, save in very exceptional cases, the rabbis could not force the husband to grant a divorce against his will. So, without the husband's agreement, wives were doomed to stay in a loveless marriage, or live alone without support and in enforced celibacy. They were labelled *agunot* – chained women. This power of Orthodox husbands has continued even into modern times, when civil divorce has become an option. In Orthodox Jewish law, civil divorce is only valid if a religious divorce has also taken place. If this did not happen, and if the woman remarried in a civil ceremony, it would count as bigamy in Jewish law. In addition, any children resulting from the second marriage would be considered illegitimate and subject to severe penalties (which will be discussed in a few pages).

Natalie's marriage turned sour after twenty-two years, but her husband refused to countenance a divorce:

> He said he wanted to make the marriage work, but I had had enough and saw no hope of improvement. Despite me leaving the family home, he insisted the marriage

was not over. I was able to eventually gain a civil divorce after suing for unreasonable behaviour, but not a religious one. I appealed to the rabbi of the congregation to which we belonged, asking him to intervene. He did arrange a meeting with my, by then, ex-husband, but my ex refused to budge and the rabbi told me that he was unable to override my ex-husband's wishes. At the time, I was irked but not very bothered as I had no intention of remarrying. Four years later, though, having met someone else and deciding to remarry – I was blocked. I still could not obtain my bullying ex's permission. It meant that my new partner and I could not have the synagogue wedding we wanted, so we were forced to settle for an impersonal registry office wedding. I am very happily married now, but I resent the idea that I am still married religiously to my first husband. It's madness, and it means I can't get him out of my life fully and move on.

Lauren told almost exactly the same story – as can countless other Jewish women – except that, in Lauren's case, the loss of a synagogue wedding was very significant for her:

To me, a registry office wedding was very second best. I wanted a sense of God's blessing on my marriage, which had been important first time round, and was even more so this time as it had gone wrong before, and I wanted to make this one the one that worked.

In Lauren's case, her rabbi had been sympathetic but unable to do anything in the face of her husband's refusal to grant the Jewish divorce. Jenny's story was even more outrageous, for her first marriage broke down after only a short period, and she was young enough to have children by the time she got remarried.

> I implored the rabbi to persuade my husband to grant the religious divorce, as I didn't want any future children tainted by the stigma of illegitimacy. I felt I had a very strong case, as my husband had left me for another woman and was clearly committing adultery, but the rabbi said that, despite this, he was powerless to act without my husband's consent. It became utterly ridiculous when my husband then chose to remarry in a registry office but still refused me a religious divorce. How on earth could that be justified! Once again, I was told nothing could be done to help me.

The rabbis were aware of the injustice of the situation but, being Orthodox, felt they lacked the authority to overturn the existing tradition. A previous Chief Rabbi of Orthodox Jewry in Britain, Joseph Hertz, even admitted that 'in the case of the *agunah*, Jewish law suffers from arrested development'[1] but felt unable to do anything about it. The only practical response was the suggestion by some rabbis that a man's wife 'should make it worth his while' by paying a sum of money to obtain the Jewish divorce. It amounted to bribery, and was being religiously condoned.

The crescendo of complaints by women led Reform rabbis to take a different course of action. It was decided

---

1   Opening Address to the Conference of Anglo-Jewish Preachers, 14 July 1925; in J.H. Hertz, *Sermons, Addresses and Studies Vol. 2* (1938, London: Soncino Press), p.13.

that an immoral law should not be part of Jewish law. The male-centred control in the time of biblical divorces had no bearing on how modern Jewish life should be conducted. Tradition was important, but should not be maintained if it was causing emotional harm or practical impediments. To summarise this in a pithy phrase, 'the past has a vote, but not a veto'. As British law means that all divorces have to be granted through the civil courts before they can be granted by the religious ones, it was deemed that, from then on, there would be no justification for a husband to refuse to grant a wife a Jewish divorce if a civil divorce had been obtained. If he did so, then the Reform *Beit Din* (rabbinic court) would override the husband's refusal, by awarding the Jewish divorce on its own authority and allowing the woman to remarry in synagogue if she so wished.

For Judith, this was a dream come true:

> I have spent the last twelve years feeling trapped by a man who ceased loving me a long time ago. He was financially abusive and has been using *halakhah* [Jewish law] to punish me for taking the kids and leaving him. He remains an angry man and he wants to hurt me. I feel so lucky to have found a way to remove his control – thank God for my new rabbi and her sensitivity!

The Orthodox reaction has been to condemn this change as a violation of Jewish law, but without suggesting any remedy for the plight of those women trapped by that same Jewish law. There was an attempt by another former Chief Rabbi, Jonathan Sacks, to lessen the problem by suggesting that all couples who married under the auspices of Orthodox synagogues should sign a form promising to come to the Orthodox *Beit Din* to discuss how best to proceed should the marriage be at breaking point. This approach was so concerned with avoiding any suggestion of coercion that it did not even mention the granting of a religious divorce. Although the attempt was noble in its intention, in practice it was seriously flawed. It was offered to couples, but was not obligatory for them to sign. It caused discomfort to individuals who had come to discuss their wedding, but found they were also being asked to think about possible termination. There is also a question mark as to how enforceable such an agreement would be, as it has never been tested in the courts.

In addition, the agreement did nothing to help all the couples who were already married. The biggest problem, though, was that it tackled the symptoms, not the disease, surrounding Jewish divorce. The obvious solution was to change Jewish law on divorce, not try to circumvent its effects. It was akin to asking drivers of unroadworthy cars to drive slowly, rather than banning them from driving in the first place.

For Reform Jews, the problem of the chained wife has been solved, and men who refuse to award a divorce, either out of malice or for financial gain, are no longer given the power to do so. Those who become ex-wives in civil law are no longer chained by Jewish law, so they are able to feel released from an unhappy relationship. They can also remarry in a Reform synagogue if they so wish. Returning to Jenny, whose former husband had already remarried civilly: eventually, she approached a Reform rabbi after being unable to obtain her Jewish divorce via the Orthodox:

He looked at me in amazement and said 'What possible reason is there for not awarding it to you?' and sent the case to the Reform *Beit Din*. They duly approached my ex, and he refused as he had done before, but this time his refusal was overturned, and the divorce awarded. I don't have a new partner, so that was not my motive – it was to be emotionally free, free of him, free of the past and not still tied to a marriage long over.

Jenny's story turned out well in the end, but she should not have been placed under the control of her ex-husband in the first place, nor endured such a tortuous and upsetting process to gain her freedom. Much sadder are the many other Jennys who have been unable to loosen their chains. It has stained their lives and has been a scar on Jewish values.

The *mamzers*

A *mamzer* is an illegitimate child. In English law, a child is illegitimate if it is born out of wedlock, but in Jewish law that is not the case, providing both parents are unmarried. In that instance, there is no blot on the status of the child, as it is deemed to be the couple's legitimate offspring, irrespective of whether or not they choose to get married. Instead, an illegitimate child in Jewish law is one that is the product of a relationship that should never have taken place, because it broke the laws on forbidden relationships. This would include a child born as a result of incest or adultery. This goes back to the Bible where, as a way of trying to prevent such unions happening, not only were the offenders punished but severe penalties were put on any child arising from the union.

According to Deuteronomy 23:3: 'A *mamzer* shall not enter in the congregation of the Eternal, nor his descendants for ten generations'. In subsequent rabbinic literature, this was taken to indicate that one who is labelled a *mamzer* could not marry a fellow Jew unless he or she was also a *mamzer*. It meant that the guilt of the man and woman cascaded down the generations and blighted the lives of those who might be living over two hundred years after the original act of immorality, yet were still made to suffer for it. In the days when prohibitions against incest and adultery were first being introduced – perhaps against the cultural norms of the time – this may have been a valid shock tactic to change communal behaviour. But however righteous the motive, it resulted in innocent people being punished for the misdeeds of relatives who lived long before they were born. As well as the public disgrace, there was a terrible practical consequence: having to find another *mamzer* to marry meant that the pool of partners available was severely curtailed.

The rabbis, themselves, recognised this but felt unable to overturn what, for them, was a divine command. In pre-modern times when records were sparse, and communication was inefficient, the more sympathetic rabbis told individuals caught in that situation to move to a different area where they were not known and could be free of the stigma. They were at least trying to be helpful, even if they could not change the root cause. In modern times, however, attitudes hardened, perhaps in response to a more sexually lax secular society and the rabbis feeling that strict measures were needed to reinforce moral standards. Astonishingly, instead of seeking to change the law, or at least mitigate its effects on innocent victims, there were attempts by some Orthodox authorities to strengthen it by compiling a list of all those who were known to be a *mamzer* and circulating it worldwide. The unofficial backdoor opportunity to escape detection was being decisively slammed shut.

For Isaac, this was hugely distressing:

> My great grandmother's husband went missing in the Boer War. After five years the authorities pronounced him dead and my great grandmother was allowed to remarry. One day, three years after that, her first husband returned. According to my grandmother, who was only a child of two at the time, the events of that day were terrible. After that my grandmother and her baby brother were both called a *mamzer*. That label has stuck and to this day it haunts me and my family.

For Reform rabbis, the very concept of the *mamzer* was an anathema. Adultery and incest were to be condemned, but the culprits were the ones to blame, not the offspring. Punishing the children – and descendants down to the tenth generation – was as immoral as the original act itself. There was also the injustice of a *mamzer* resulting from the chained wife situation mentioned above: if a woman who had a civil divorce but whose husband refused to grant a religious one were to remarry, the second marriage would be invalid in Jewish law as she would still be seen as tied to her first husband; the second marriage would therefore count as adultery and any children would be given the status of a *mamzer*. Once again, Reform rabbis felt impelled to act to change a monstrously unfair Jewish law. In a radical move, the category of a *mamzer* was deemed to be no longer in existence. The opprobrium for adultery and incest remained, but it would have no impact on the status of any children. It was seen not so much as a matter of bringing Jewish law in line with secular standards, but of making Jewish law consistent with its own morality.

Naturally, this unilateral move was vigorously opposed by the Orthodox rabbinate. To be fair, they fully understood the moral problem, but felt that a biblical law was a divine law and so could not be altered. Yes, it may cause hardship, they argued, but there was an overall divine plan that we humans could not always fathom. For Reform rabbis, though, this was an example of moral cowardice. There were other biblical laws that had been dropped because of 'the needs of the time', such as the injunction that all debts should be acquitted every seven years, which had led to people refusing to give loans lest they not be repaid. Other laws had been nullified through interpretation. Thus the very literal verse in Exodus 21:24 about 'an eye for an eye and a tooth for a tooth' was instead viewed as compensatory in subsequent rabbinic literature: 'an eye's *worth* for an eye and a tooth's *worth* for a tooth'. The case of the *mamzer* could have received similar treatment. In the absence of any attempt to do so for several centuries, it was now felt that it was time to label it as, at best, inappropriate and, at worst, un-Jewish, and abolish it altogether.

Inevitably, very few people admit to being a *mamzer* because of the aspersions it casts on their family. Jeffrey, however, had no choice:

When my fiancée and I went to our local Orthodox rabbi to arrange a marriage, the interview went fine and plans for our special day seemed to progress smoothly. Two weeks later, I received a phone call from the rabbi, asking me to come and discuss 'a complication' that had arisen. At the first interview, I had been asked to prove my Jewish status by providing my mother's *ketubbah*, the document of Jewish marriage, which would have been proof that she was Jewish and therefore I was too. At the time, I said that I was unable to do so as my mother had had a civil wedding and so I offered alternative proof instead, which was accepted. However, on checking records, the rabbi had discovered that my mother had not been able to obtain a Jewish divorce from her first husband before marrying her second husband, my father.

The rabbi tried to put it as diplomatically as he could: 'It means that technically your mother was still married to her previous husband when she married your father, which made it bigamy and counts as an adulterous relationship. So you are what we call a *mamzer* and cannot marry anyone other than another *mamzer*, and so your wedding cannot proceed. I am very sorry, but we'll have to call it off.' At first, I felt devastated, both to learn of a family problem of which I had been unaware, and to be told that I could not get married. But that very quickly turned to anger. What right had the rabbi to destroy two young people's lives because of something written some three or four thousand years ago? If he'd said he reckoned we were unsuitable for each other for some reason, I would have argued with him, but could have understood it. But this is ridiculous. And what does it achieve apart from hurting a couple who love each other and pushing us away from all things Jewish?

Although he was reluctant to expose himself to more rejection, Jeffrey was persuaded to approach a Reform synagogue and found a very different response:

> When I explained the circumstances of my mother's inability to get a Jewish divorce before marrying my dad – I wanted to get it out and be up front about it at the beginning of the conversation to save hiccups later – the rabbi didn't blink an eyelid. She just said that those things happened and were very regrettable, but it didn't affect me and started talking about setting the wedding date.

For traditionalists, Jeffrey's wedding was a travesty, for the family it was a wonderful day, and for Reform circles it was modern Judaism in action.

The priests

A simple glance through the Book of Leviticus shows how the priests dominated the religious life of that period. They alone were the ones who performed the main rites, which largely consisted of animal sacrifices or harvest offerings. It was a hereditary position, starting with Aaron and his sons, and then extending through the male line to their children and all subsequent descendants. Initially, sacrifices were performed wherever the Israelites were encamped during the forty years wandering in the wilderness, but they later become centralised in the Temple in Jerusalem and could not be done elsewhere. The priestly rituals continued until the destruction of the Temple during the conquest of Jerusalem by the Romans in the year 70 CE. With their role gone and their base destroyed, the religious leadership quickly changed to the rabbis. It was they who led the prayers and the textual study that took place in synagogues scattered throughout the country. These had already begun developing during Temple times, but since the destruction had become the main focus of public worship. However, the status of a person being a priest (also known as a *cohen*) was still recognised on the basis that the Temple might be rebuilt at some period, in which case they would be needed to service it again. As the centuries progressed, this hope became ever more unlikely, especially after the Al Aqsa mosque was built on the same site in the eighth century.

The active role of priests was considerably reduced: they had the kudos of being the first person called to the Reading of the Scrolls in services. They were called upon to bless the congregation on particular occasions, and participated in ceremonies on the birth of a first-born boy. There were also various prohibitions that affected priests, and these too were maintained: they could not come into contact with a dead body and they could not marry a divorcee. The former meant that they had to keep to the public paths of a cemetery and sit in a special area of the prayer hall, a slight inconvenience but not very onerous. The latter was much more of a problem, as Esther found out. She had been divorced before meeting Roy. Her joy at his proposal of marriage quickly evaporated when his rabbi explained that as Roy had inherited the status of priest, the two of them could not be wed. To her amazement, he suggested that the two of them 'put it behind you and instead go and meet someone else'. Roy had always known he was a priest, but had never realised it carried this bar: 'But I've never acted as a priest, and probably never will, so what difference does marrying Esther make?' The rabbi was adamant that nothing could proceed, even when Roy offered to renounce his status as a priest. Esther was less measured:

> I can't believe that a rule made for people who were religious leaders in ancient times still applies to a descendant two thousand years later. That's utterly mad.

The rabbi chose not to comment, but indicated that the interview was at an end. It was partly for the sake of couples such as Esther and Roy that Reform rabbis decided to abolish the category of being a priest. It was not only that it denied couples happiness, but it was based on assumptions that were no longer valid. It assumed that there was a stigma attached to a divorced woman (see Chapter 10), and also that marrying her would taint the purity of priests and render them unable to perform their religious duties properly.

There were two other objections. One was that the priesthood was effectively a caste system, based not on merit but on birth. The Reform response was that this should have no place in a faith that regarded all people as equal, both generally and religiously. The inference that some Jews were inherently more holy than other Jews was not acceptable. The second objection was that the priesthood was based on the sacrificial system. Not only was it relegated to the past, but Reform rabbis wanted it to remain that way. Whereas the daily and Sabbath Orthodox service calls for the restoration of the Temple and the resumption of animal sacrifices, the Reform liturgy does not do so. There is no desire to see their return, so it would be unthinkable to pray for it, which is why there is no logic in maintaining the role of those who once performed sacrifices. It would be as politically outrageous as Parliament paying for the upkeep of an official hangman despite the death penalty being abolished.

Once again, as in the case of the chained wife and *mamzer*, the Orthodox authorities felt that Reform was acting unilaterally, without authority and undermining Judaism. For the Reform, it was remedying a problem that should have been tackled centuries earlier, it was behaving in accordance with Jewish values and it was enhancing Jewish life. Certainly, Esther and Roy would agree. They approached a Reform synagogue, were told that his ancestry had no bearing on whom he could choose to marry and they now have two children together.

In Reform synagogues today, any member of the community can be called up first to the Reading of the Scrolls, the person leading the service gives the blessing and firstborn boys are no longer singled out for special treatment over any other siblings. The abolition of the priesthood was primarily a matter of principle, but was also done with a keen eye on its negative effects on Jewish life.

3

Realistic Religion

Time for Judaism to address today's needs, or risk oblivion

There was a time when intelligent people parked their cognitive abilities and rational principles at the door of the house of worship. Perhaps many are still content to do so, and unquestioningly accept doctrines which, if they passed across their work desk, they would subject to rigorous scrutiny and probably dismiss. It is the very nature of faith, they would argue, that makes certain ideas exempt from normal probing, and they are happy simply to believe.

However, many are no longer prepared to suspend their critical faculties in that way. It is one of the reasons why the Church of England has lost so many adherents, who find they cannot relate to what seem to them to be bizarre concepts: a virgin who conceives, a man-god, a deity who not only dies but is resurrected for a short while and then disappears for over two thousand years.

The same religious rebellion has been happening within the Jewish world. Items of faith that have not been challenged for centuries are no longer viewed as 'the gospel truth'. That very phrase – now used ironically rather than emphatically – indicates how the unconditional acceptance of former years has long disappeared.

Honest prayer

In response, Reform synagogues have adopted the principle of religious honesty: that those coming to services should not be asked to say prayers in which they do not believe. It is not appropriate to keep the traditional text of previous generations and expect worshippers to skip over sentences to which they cannot sign up, a form of staccato prayer, yet still find it meaningful.

The result is that references to a variety of concepts and practices have been excised from the liturgy. One is the resurrection of the dead, which is nothing to do with Jesus but is based on the passage in Ezekiel about a valley of dry bones which come to life (37:1–6) and gradually evolved into the notion that, at some point, all those who had died would return to life. It is hardly a credible belief: think about the overcrowding! And at what age would the deceased all return – at the time of death when many were in their dotage, mentally or physically, and unable to even get out of bed? It is redolent of the wishful thinking of a bygone age, hoping for a second chance at life. Instead, the new liturgy has references to the fact that God 'renews life beyond death' – a deliberately open-ended phrase that can be interpreted as some form of afterlife or one's contribution to life continuing after our departure from it. The Orthodox may object that it is far too vague compared to the very exact promise of resurrection, but at least it is possibly right rather than definitely wrong.

Another omission is reference to the Messiah. Judaism certainly believes in a time when – if everyone behaved ethically – the world would be at peace, without wars or civil strife or domestic friction. It may seem a long way off, but it is possible to conceive of it occurring. It is also part of Judaism's refusal to accept the status quo: that the current version of the world has to be the final version and cannot be bettered. Unlike Christianity, though, it was not held that everything would be dependent on one individual – a deity or his son. The original Jewish idea of the Messiah was that he was a human and his arrival would be the confirmation that the world had perfected itself. However, constant references to the Messiah over the centuries, along with the influence of Christianity, led to his being seen as the prime cause rather than the final seal.

As a way of refocusing the concept, Reform liturgy has been changed to the 'messianic era', emphasising the time of harmony instead of one particular person. It also helps remind that such a time will not occur miraculously, but needs people to work towards it, thereby encouraging everyone to play their part in making it happen. Everyone's actions count. Whether we see ourselves as aid-workers in the divine plan, or fulfilling our human endeavours, we can each contribute, while our failure to act delays the process.

Animal sacrifices feature throughout the Bible, but have not been part of Jewish life since the year 70 CE when the Temple in Jerusalem was destroyed. Yet they are a common theme running through the traditional liturgy, with both references to them and prayers calling for their restoration. It is highly doubtful whether modern Orthodox Jews really want to return to a form of worship that involves killing lambs or pigeons and sprinkling their blood around the altar. But while the Orthodox will add new prayers, they rarely delete old ones. This is based on the notion that although the prayers were written by humans, and are not divine in origin, they have acquired the sanctity of time and should not be altered. Some might claim that they personally do not wish to see the return of such rituals and only include mention of them for historic purposes. But, for many modern Jews, whatever role animal sacrifices had in the past two millennia, they are definitely not appropriate today and have no place in the service. They, too, are no longer found in Reform prayer books.

For the prayers that are included in Reform liturgy, there is an issue not only of content but also of comprehension. Whereas Orthodox services are conducted entirely in Hebrew – save for the Prayer for the Royal Family – many Jews cannot read Hebrew or, if they can, do not understand it. As prayer is one of the most personal expressions of one's reflections, appreciation, hopes and fears, it is astonishing that people are expected to pray in a language that is alien to them. It would no more make sense than to agree to an interview with someone speaking to you in a foreign language of which you had no knowledge and to whose questions you could not respond. The Reform prayer book, therefore, has all prayers translated into English, with synagogues varying as to what percentage of Hebrew they use in services, but typically around 50% of each. Moreover, the English is modern English – as opposed to the King James version – so that those prayers recited in English roll off the tongue easily and do not sound as if they, too, are in a foreign language. This may seem a totally obvious development, but religion does not always go for the obvious, and there are still plenty of synagogues where worshippers either have no idea of what the exclusively Hebrew prayers mean, or simply do not bother turning up for a morning of incomprehension.

As for the songs, almost all of them are sung in Hebrew, so another recent development has been to include a transliterated version of the Hebrew in the prayer book, so that those not familiar with Hebrew can join in the more evocative parts of the service, which would otherwise be closed to them. In an ideal world, of course, all Jews would make the effort to learn Hebrew properly, but religion has to deal with the world as it is, not as it ought to be. Only then might it have any chance of nudging people from the former to the latter state of affairs.

In the same vein of thought, instrumental music has been brought back into modern services. This happened in ancient times, and the Bible often refers to the cymbals, harps, lutes, pipes, drums and other instruments that were used in the Temple in Jerusalem. However, after its destruction by the Romans in the first century, it was decreed by the rabbis that musical instruments should no longer be played. This was partly out of mourning for the loss of the Temple and partly because of Sabbath regulations. Whatever validity that may have had in the past, it was felt by Reform that the ban was vastly outweighed by the benefits that music can bring: whether creating a powerful atmosphere, encouraging communal participation or aiding periods of reflection.

Many Reform synagogues introduced organs, while it has become customary in recent years to have guitars, tambourines and bongos. If the Psalmist is right to urge us to 'serve God with joy' (100:2) – a saying that is engraved on the Ark in many synagogues – then musical accompaniment at Sabbath services may horrify those attached to bygone rules, yet it helps the modern worshipper to pray. As Keith, who considers himself 'a periodic regular', attending every six weeks, explained:

> For me, services are not just about praying with my mind, but tapping my foot and using my lungs, and unless the whole of me is involved, I feel I've been short-changed.

Another practical innovation has been to abolish the Orthodox rule about having a quorum of ten adult males (*minyan*) at services, without which certain sections cannot be said. It is a case of a good idea sometimes having unfortunate consequences. The need for a quorum encouraged the idea of communal prayer: coming to synagogue not just because you yourself want to do so, but so as to support the others there who depend on your presence to have the full service. This is highly beneficial and helps create a sense of camaraderie, especially if it is a small congregation where the requisite numbers might be in short supply. As will be seen in Chapter 7, Reform had already changed the definition of a *minyan* to include women, asserting that they are just as valid religiously as men and count equally.

However, there are occasions when, because of bad weather or other factors, it is impossible to reach the quorum and only five, six or seven people are present. In theory, the reading from the scroll should not take place, nor should the *kaddish* – the memorial prayer for those who have died – be recited. However, as these are among the most significant parts of the services, many Reform rabbis hold that it is wrong to penalise those who did bother to come because of those who are absent. They will therefore allow the full service to proceed, including a funeral one. Naturally, every rabbi wants their synagogue bursting at the seams, but if the opposite is the case for whatever reason, then it is more important to cater for the needs of those attending, rather than worry about a rites and practices rule-book.

Twenty-first century Sabbath

A similar reasoning has led to an even more novel development: live-streaming of services. For the Orthodox this is doubly forbidden: both for the synagogue to turn on the electronic equipment and for those watching it to log on to their computers, as it contravenes their understanding of Sabbath observance. However, there are many people who are very keen to attend services but cannot do so – such as those who are ill or infirm, live too far away or are carers who cannot leave the house. Why should they be denied the opportunity to benefit from the prayers and feel linked to the community? In response, therefore, many Reform synagogues have installed a live-streaming system. Fears that it might encourage some who could attend to instead take the easy route and watch from home failed to materialise, as the actual experience of being in synagogue and feeling the warmth of fellow members around you is much more compelling. However, for those previously unable to join from afar, it has proved a wonderful comfort. As Nicholas and Pearl explain:

> We live a long way from our synagogue. Since Nicholas had a stroke we have felt isolated and we so miss our old routine of attending synagogue each week. What a Godsend it was when they installed a web camera. Now, every Saturday morning, we sit down with a cup of tea and our prayer books to beam in to the service. It is

so comforting to see a familiar space, hear the familiar tunes and see some of our friends that we've known since we first joined in the 1970s. Our routine on Saturday lunchtime is to discuss the rabbi's sermon.

Modern technology may break some ancient laws, but it enhances Jewish life today, and so there is little doubt as to whether God is smiling or scowling.

The same 'get real' approach applies also to how Jews actually make their way to synagogue. This is simply not an issue for Christians and those of other faiths – you reach church or other places of worship by walking or by car or by public transport, depending on how far you live away from it and on your personal circumstances. It is purely a practical matter and nothing to do with your faith. For Orthodox Judaism, however, travelling on the Sabbath by car is strictly forbidden. This is because it counts as the type of work that is banned on the Sabbath by the Ten Commandments (Exodus 20:8). Of course, driving is not specifically mentioned in the text, but rabbinic tradition later interprets 'work' as referring to various acts, including lighting a fire. As turning on a car ignition creates an electrical spark, which is deemed akin to creating a fire, driving is banned as an extension of the original command.

On the one hand, it is almost ludicrous to base the prohibition against driving from a text written some four thousand years before cars were invented; on the other hand, there is a certain internal logic if you accept the original interpretation and take it to its ultimate conclusion. There are also some incidental benefits, such as encouraging people to live near a synagogue and fostering a sense of local community, rather than commuting from afar and feeling disconnected.

However, these bonuses are more than outweighed by the negative impact on those who do not live within walking distance, or are infirm, or are bringing children. They either have to stay at home and miss out on communal participation or they have to cheat by parking a few streets away from the synagogue where they cannot be detected, and pretend they have walked the whole distance. Such behaviour not only brings Jewish law into disrepute, but is a terrible example to one's children, who grow up learning religious deception from their parents.

Reform rabbis have therefore taken it upon themselves to redefine what 'work' means and what the injunction does and does not cover. The principle of not doing one's usual tasks on the Sabbath is maintained, so that the day is special and can be set aside for personal refreshment. Collecting wood and lighting a fire in ancient times may have been laborious, as would have been saddling one's donkey for a journey and bumping along unmade roads, but neither applies today. A car facilitates coming to services and being part of the community.

Reform rabbis therefore hold that there are no modern objections to driving. In fact, it is irrelevant how one gets to synagogue – what counts is being there. The result is that Reform synagogue car parks are open for congregants to use on the Sabbath. Some might consider it bizarre that Orthodox ones are closed at a time when they are needed most, but perhaps a sign saying 'Closed – no entry' is an apt image for a much wider message to modernity.

At the same time, in a fast-paced world of emails and social media, many Reform rabbis are reclaiming the Sabbath by urging their congregants to take a weekly break from their work and enjoy a pause from slaving over their inboxes and smartphones. Of course, there is nothing wrong with using technology on the Sabbath for recreational purposes, such as watching football or playing an e-game of Scrabble with a relative in Australia, but the essence of the Sabbath is about creating a sacred, stress-free hiatus in one's working week. In this way, and in so many others, Reform rabbis are adapting ancient ideas to a modern world.

Re-evaluating the *Torah*

This willingness by Reform rabbis to adapt biblical rules to everyday life is predicated on a distinctive approach to the text itself. For the Orthodox, the *Torah* (the Five Books of Moses) is the word of God, relayed to humans through Moses. If this view is accepted, then it is the most powerful text ever written, for nothing can be more precious than the literal word of God. It therefore has binding authority, is unchangeable and cannot be ignored or contradicted. By contrast, Reform sees the *Torah* as a marriage between God and humans. Like any relationship, this marriage evolves over time, so Jewish law is part divine revelation, part human inspiration and part the refinements of subsequent generations who handed down the text till it reached its current form.

The *Torah* contains both material of eternal value (such as not committing adultery) and extracts that are limited to a particular era (such as not mixing linen and wool together). What is crucial is the task of sifting between the divine and the time-bound, and distinguishing between what is of value and what is irrelevant or even counter-productive. Each generation has to find the voice of God speaking within the text and apply it to the challenges they face. For the Orthodox, this is heresy; for the Reform, it is common sense.

The key principle of this approach is the right to change. It empowers us to say that a law is no longer appropriate, such as that preventing a divorcee marrying a *cohen* (see Chapters 2 and 10), rather than defending it or circumventing it. Similarly, it permits us to depart from rabbinic interpretations of a text, such as not driving on the Sabbath, when either the interpretation was flawed or circumstances have changed. The Bible and rabbinic tradition are still the starting point, but not necessarily the final word. As the saying quoted earlier puts it, 'the past has a vote, but not a veto.'

If an attitude of 'sceptical respect' applies to the laws of the *Torah*, a similar approach is adopted towards the narrative aspects. The opening chapters of the Book of Genesis are seen not as a scientific analysis of how the world began, but as a poetic attempt to explain the inexplicable. Whereas many Orthodox Jews will assert that the world was indeed created in six days, Reform prefer to talk about six eras or stages (concerning which Genesis and science seem to concur): light, matter, sea life, land vegetation, animal life, human life.

Yet, what really matters is the notion that humanity stems from the same source, and therefore everyone is equal and should be treated with respect. There is also the implication that the world has a purpose, that life matters and that individuals count. Equally important is the fact that humans are the last in the chain of creation and therefore have a responsibility to sustain the world they have inherited. Thus, even if the Genesis account is not factually correct, it can still contain many truths.

The same applies to the rest of Genesis. The Tower of Babel is almost certainly not the reason why people today speak different languages, but it does highlight how lack of communication can cause division. A precondition for bringing about harmony is to ensure that opposing parties understand each other's perspective. Noah may have been a fictional character, but the way the world so often teeters on the brink of destruction is a warning that constantly needs reinforcing, not least in an age of consumerism versus conservation.

The saga of Jacob and his family is a case study of a dysfunctional family, with parental favouritism and sibling rivalry leading to catastrophic consequences. Amid it all, there are individuals struggling to rise above their circumstances, and often having to go on a journey in order to achieve the new life of which they dream. Some journeys are successful, whilst others are not; learning to live with one's limitations and failures can be as powerful as admiring the success stories.

The significance of the Genesis narratives is not whether they are true or not, but whether they have value for those reading them now. There is also the constant God-thread running throughout the book. Sometimes God is in search of particular characters, whether they want it or not; other times, they are in search of God. Both scenarios can resonate with us today. The ability to learn from Genesis without believing in it is the same reason why one can be religious without being fundamentalist.

Keeping *kosher*

A practical consequence of this approach can be seen in the Reform approach to the dietary laws (*kashrut*) and keeping *kosher*. As everyone knows, Jews do not eat pork, although there are a variety of other forbidden foods listed in the Bible, from rabbits to shellfish to insects. However, subsequent rabbinic tradition extended these prohibitions to not mixing meat and milk products in the same meal. This would preclude having ice-cream after roast beef, or white coffee after lamb chops.

These restrictions were further extended to keeping separate cooking utensils, crockery and cutlery for milk and meat dishes. It dates from an age in which many pots and bowls were porous and so particles from a previous meal might become absorbed, with the result that meat and milk were inadvertently mixed together. Realistically, these problems are unlikely in the time of glazed crockery and the use of dishwashers. Still, such rituals can be helpful as a form of religious identity or as reminders of wider Jewish values. However, they can be problematic if one is living and working within society at large. It is certainly possible to avoid the forbidden foods when eating at a restaurant or visiting the home of non-Jewish friends. However, it is highly problematic if one insists on separate crockery and cutlery that has only been used for meat or milk dishes.

Reform takes the view that being *kosher* is not an 'all or nothing' observance, in which one has to keep every aspect or be in breach of it. Instead, there are degrees, and individuals can choose their own level within it. Synagogues may choose to keep all aspects so that no one attending worries about the state of the food, but it is not for rabbis to legislate as to members' fridges and cupboards. Many Reform Jews, therefore, will abstain from pork and other foods, but not make distinctions over the crockery. It enables them to maintain an important ritual, but does not prevent them from socialising with non-Jews over a meal. Moreover, many Reform Jews return to the essence of the *kosher* rules – that by not cooking a kid in its own mother's milk (repeated three time in the *Torah* in Exodus 23:19, 34:26 and Deuteronomy 14:21) they are commanded to avoid any unnecessary animal suffering or cruelty. Therefore, many Reform Jews adhere to eco-*kashrut*, by which traditional dietary laws are extended to prioritising fair trade, free-range, organic, non-genetically modified products over heavily processed, strictly *kosher* food while others choose to be vegetarian.

Sex and death

Another issue that highlights the need to accommodate the way modern Jews lead their lives is that a high percentage of couples live together before marriage. In some Jewish circles this is considered highly inappropriate. Whereas, Reform rabbis accept that it is virtually the norm today. What is important is not the date at which they have sex – before or after the wedding – but the quality of the relationship, and whether it is a stable and loving partnership.

A closely linked issue is that of contraception and protective sex. Contraception is allowed in Jewish law, but, based on the verse in Genesis 38:9–10, it was considered heinous to 'spill one's seed' or engage in 'Onanism'. This led to forms of contraception being permitted that did not interrupt a man's seed from entering a woman's vagina, such as the pill or diaphragm or IUD. However, those that did prevent it, such as condoms, were strictly forbidden.

Reform, though, has elected to depart from this ban. This was initially because of the view that life in the modern world should not necessarily be governed by rules developed four millennia ago. These rules need to be considered, but can be jettisoned if no longer appropriate. This permission – seen as a matter of principle – has become even more significant for practical reasons ever since the arrival of AIDS. Once it became known that condoms had protective value, then not only did Reform rabbis permit them, but actively urged their use as a life-saving procedure. This was in stark contrast to the Orthodox, who said that the ban on condoms had to be maintained, whatever the consequences.

The Orthodox rabbinate added that the way to avoid catching the life-threatening disease was for heterosexuals to have sex only within marriage, and for homosexuals not to have sex at all. In theory, this would help avoid anyone falling prey to AIDS. In reality, however, sexual mores were not going to change: sex before marriage is now common, as is having several sexual partners, be it in succession or at the same time. In addition, the LGBT+ world, having only just been liberated (see Chapter 9), was not going to be told to hide away and opt for abstinence. The condom question has been a stark illustration of the difference between those who wish to minister to the world as they believe it should be, and those who try to minister to the world as it actually is.

A similar principle of adapting to reality applies when dealing with a death. Until recently, cremation was viewed with horror within Jewish circles and burials were the norm. The objection was that cremation destroyed the body. This was seen as both insulting to the deceased and disrespectful to the divinely created body that had once housed the soul. However, modern cremations are conducted with the utmost respect and decorum, and almost always at the request of the person concerned. Another cause for disapproval was that, in view of the Orthodox belief in the physical resurrection of the body and soul in the messianic age, it was held that if the body was burnt, then the soul could not reunite with it, and so the person would not be resurrected.

As seen earlier in the chapter, Reform thinking does not hold to this belief, and so the objection is invalid. Even if some individuals do believe in resurrection, then once one is in the realm of the miraculous, anything can happen. So, if decomposed bones can be resurrected, then why not dead ashes? Cremation is therefore viewed within Reform as a perfectly appropriate option for those who so wish and a matter of personal choice. The service itself is exactly the same as at a burial, with the familiar prayers that can be comforting to mourners. It is a good example of a modern innovation conducted in a traditional manner, marrying past and present.

Access for all

A very different aspect of being realistic includes the need for religion to be accessible. Orthodox synagogues that place women upstairs create a problem for those unable to manage stairs. Having men and women all together on the same ground floor means that Reform synagogues obviate this problem. As was seen above, the Orthodox prohibition against travelling on the Sabbath prevents anyone with infirmities or disabilities attending services, and this has also been solved by Reform re-assessing what is and is not prohibited. The use of a loop-system for hearing aids may be questioned by some for the same reason, but is considered inconsequential by Reform in the light of the benefits it can bring. A similar green light is given to the use of electric wheelchairs, and even non-electric wheelchairs, prams and buggies in areas where Orthodox Judaism prohibits them being pushed to the synagogue on the Sabbath. In a desire to make Judaism accessible to all, irrespective of whether they arrive on two legs or four wheels, many Reform synagogues have built ramps to facilitate entry and exit.

If those with physical issues need to be made welcome, the same applies to those with poor mental health (see also Chapter 10). This includes not just tolerating those concerned, but also finding positive roles for them to occupy and feel valued. This might involve allocating tasks that not only suit their abilities, but also give them responsibilities in a safe environment. It might range from being in charge of certain duties in the garden to helping at the elderly Friendship Club. Just as importantly, the rest of the community needs to see them as fellow-members, not as charity cases. It may be that some need professional help, but it is enormously beneficial that, when they leave the counselling room or care home, they can go to 'their community', a place where they are recognised, feel comfortable and have a part to play. As Sammy put it:

> I like coming to the synagogue. The rabbi always says 'Hello, Sammy' – he knows my name! I work in the library for two hours every week, helping to repair the books. No one has their own seat in synagogue, but when I go I like to sit in the same place. Once I got there late and someone was in my seat, so I asked them to move and they did.

Sammy has now left that synagogue, as the residential home in which he lived has been relocated. But the synagogue has honoured his contribution by calling its social outreach programme 'Sammy's seat'.

In a world where institutions can struggle to address the needs of the individual, it is the values of autonomy, inclusivity and intellectual integrity that make the Reform synagogue a welcoming place where one can realistically embrace all the religious advantages and challenges of living in a modern world.

Climate change

Reform synagogues were among the first to respond positively to the warnings about global warming. They chimed with numerous rabbinic injunctions from earlier centuries to nurture the earth – seeing humans as tenants in God's world, not owners, with a duty to hand it on intact to future generations. This in turn was based on the biblical command 'not to destroy' life-sustaining aspects of the environment (Deuteronomy 20:19).

As a result, Reform synagogues have adopted many practical ways to save energy (installing solar panels and low energy lights), avoid waste (using china crockery rather than disposable plates and cups), save resources (buying recycled paper, changing to dual flush toilets and composting food waste). They have also encouraged their members to do likewise in their own homes and places of work. While many people would see this as a common sense approach to a climate emergency, for Reform Jews it is also a religious responsibility and part of our duty to ensure that we protect God's creation.

4

Atheist Jews

Why Jewish unbelievers are so many and still Jewish

For some, the phrase 'atheist Jew' is an oxymoron: Jews believe in God, so someone who does not think God exists cannot be Jewish. In reality, though, the phrase describes a new category of Jews that has emerged in recent times. They are like Robin, a business manager in his fifties who had a fairly traditional Jewish upbringing, and is now a convinced atheist:

> It's very simple. I see no evidence for a God, either in the creation of the world or in the way it has developed. I don't mind other people believing in God if that makes sense to them, but it certainly doesn't for me.

However, that has not stopped him remaining a member of a synagogue:

> I may not believe Jewish, but I am still Jewish, subscribe to Jewish values and want to remain part of the community.

He participates in social and cultural events, pays his annual subscription and goes to the occasional service for family events. He sees no contradiction between his Jewish identity and his lack of belief.

If Robin had come from a Christian background that would probably have been the end of his association with the Church. A Christian atheist – who does not acknowledge the Father, Son and Holy Ghost – would find the Church had little to offer him or her. Judaism, however, has always been much more than a faith. Clearly, it is based on a deity who communicated with Abraham, spoke with Moses, took the Israelites out of Egypt, revealed the Ten Commandments at Mount Sinai and brought the Israelites to the Promised Land.

But at the same time, the fact that one is born a Jew – coming from Jewish parentage – means that one is automatically Jewish and needs no declaration of faith or act of affirmation later on. You are Jewish whether you practise it or not. A Jew who is not circumcised and lacks the initiation rite for boys is an uncircumcised Jew, but still a Jew. Even Jews who convert to another religion still technically never lose their Jewish status. They are simply apostate Jews. The adjective may change, but the noun does not.

There are also many Jews who are not certain what they believe. They are fairly sure that they cannot sign up to the God of the prayer book, but do not dismiss the idea of a God/creative force still existing. As Fran explained:

There's no way that I think the Power that created the world billions of year ago will listen to my puny prayers

or even have any interest in my existence. So, the service
doesn't make much sense to me, but I don't rule out there
being a God in some other way.

Yet Fran, and others who describe themselves as agnostic,
still believe in the Jewish community and want to continue
the Jewish heritage in other respects.

Until recently, Robin and Fran would not have been
able to voice their disbelief and doubts within a synagogue
context. In fact, when Robin did feel confident enough to
approach his Orthodox rabbi to discuss the matter, he was
told that his atheism was just a passing phase, and that he
should keep coming to services, for eventually he would
find God again:

> What really annoyed me was the inability to understand
> that I wasn't being daft or difficult, but had come to an
> informed position that differed from that of the rabbi.

When Robin told his rabbi that there was no point
continuing to come to services if God did not exist, he
was told that he'd better stay away until he regained his
faith. Robin reckoned that the rabbi was afraid he would
be a bad influence on others. Robin duly resigned and only
joined a Reform synagogue ten years later when a friend
persuaded him that he would receive a different response:

> I was very dubious at first, but was taken aback when the
> rabbi said that his synagogue was full of atheists and
> agnostics, but he didn't care, as there were different ways
> of being Jewish and they still had a strong Jewish identity.

The rabbi showed Robin the *kosher* shop that the synagogue ran on its premises, which stocked Jewish foods that were not available in the local stores, such as viennas, worsht, chopped liver, heimishe cucumber, and explained:

> We have lots of members who won't be seen dead in services on a Saturday, but religiously come every Sunday to the shop, because they don't pray Jewish but they eat Jewish. But that's ok, it's all part of being a community.

Robin decided to join when the rabbi went on to say:

> I genuinely don't care whether people come to services, or the adult education, or the book circle, or the film evening, or the lunches for the homeless – it's keeping the umbilical cord with Judaism going, in whatever way you choose.

Lucy, though, did not find such a warm welcome. When she told fellow members of her synagogue she was an atheist, she was told that Jews of the past had died to keep the faith alive and she was throwing away their sacrifice. Increasingly, she felt estranged from others:

> I felt everyone was talking about me behind my back. I hadn't eaten a pork chop or covered the synagogue walls with graffiti, just voiced my personal opinion, but it was as if I was the Number One sinner. In the end I decided I didn't fit in, and just left. I had enough to do with my job and various interests, but I was sorry it ended so unpleasantly. I still see my Jewish friends socially, but not in communal settings and have drifted from any

organised involvement with Jewish life. But what I really resented was that others felt the same way, but didn't express it.

Lucy's case highlights the fact that Jews who have problems with 'the God bit' are far from isolated individuals, and are probably much greater in number than most rabbis care to admit.

The God problem

In some ways, the problem is endemic to Judaism. God is taken for granted at the very beginning of the Bible, with Genesis 1:1 declaring that 'In the beginning God created the heavens and the earth...'. The focus of interest is thenceforth not God, but humanity. The Hebrew Bible does not bother to explore the nature of God, but concentrates on how people should behave. Whereas the Catholic key text is the Nicene Creed and the Church of England has its Thirty-Nine Articles of Faith, Judaism has the Ten Commandments (or six hundred and thirteen commandments if the whole Pentateuch is taken into account). It is primarily *doing*, rather than *believing*.

It is extraordinary that the first accepted summary of Jewish beliefs – Moses Maimonides' Thirteen Principles of Jewish Faith – was not written until the twelfth century. Of course, there were beliefs long before then, but it had never been considered necessary, or desirable, to codify them. It was as if belief, like sex, was too personal a subject to talk about in public. It was assumed, but never debated. Individual Jews may have had their own views or formulations, but provided that the idea of God was accepted – a God who created the world and then periodically intervened in it – there was little interest as to any further details about the nature of God. However, once attempts at codifying the characteristics of God were undertaken, there was an obligation to adhere to them or be accused of not being properly Jewish.

According to the Thirteen Principles enunciated by Maimonides, a view generally accepted by other Jewish authorities, God is an indivisible unity, is incorporeal, is beyond time, is solely responsible for the world, gave the Law to Moses, knows all human thoughts, rewards and punishes, and will ultimately bring about the resurrection of the dead. Moreover, each of these assertions is prefaced with the words 'I believe with perfect faith that...'. Prior to this point, rabbis had been much more concerned with actions rather than policing what Jews thought. Unlike Christianity, the heretic in Judaism was not the person who believed the wrong thing, but the person who did the wrong thing.

Even Jews who fervently believe in God can legitimately have radically varying images of God in their own mind. For some, God is the scriptwriter who controls our very movements according to a predetermined, or pre-envisaged, plan. We exist in a world where God's will, understood or not, is crucial. For others, God is the engineer who created the world and now lets it run according to its own devices. God has stepped back and looks on from afar as to how it manages by itself. For others, God is the check-out-till supervisor who lets humans do what they want in the supermarket of life, but then tots up the bill and judges them at the exit. We have complete freedom throughout our life, but a final reckoning is unavoidable at the end. For others, God is the still, small voice that is our conscience. It gives us a sense of how to behave, and how not to behave, although whether we listen to it is another matter. For yet others, God is the force of nature that ensures the sun rises each day, the seasons change and we can exist in a habitable world. There is regularity and rhythm, and we can make plans, have children and expect there to be a tomorrow. Several of these images are incompatible with each other, but they are all equally Jewish. They attest to the unimportance of theological consistency in Judaism compared to some other faiths.

It is no accident that the over-simplified but telling summary of where Judaism and Christianity differ is that 'Judaism is a religion of deed, Christianity is a religion of creed'. In essence, theology is a Christian sport rather than a Jewish one. When discussing a new book on Judaism in 1990, the then Bishop of Oxford, Richard Harries said: 'This is a typically Jewish book, with 280 pages on what to do and 20 on what to believe. If it was a Christian book, it would be the other way round.'

Nevertheless, many rabbis feel caught out by the growing numbers of Jews willing to express their religious doubts. The emphasis of rabbinic training has been to remind Jews to maintain observances – be it keeping the Sabbath, eating *kosher* or marrying within the faith – but theology has never been a priority. For some, the answer is to insist on the centrality of God and that anyone who denies God is indulging in religious misbehaviour. After all, if there is not a God who has commanded that we adhere to the observances, then why bother keeping them? Others dismiss belief as a very personal matter, not for public scrutiny. For them, what is important is communal participation. Working out one's own beliefs is secondary and is something over which one can take one's time. When Fran spoke to her minister about feeling hypocritical about being both an agnostic and yet a member of the Synagogue Council, she was firmly told:

> A hypocrite is someone who dissembles and pretends. You are being perfectly honest about where you stand, so I have no problem with that, and see no reason for you to resign.

When she discussed it with her rabbi a year later, he asked if her thoughts had changed, and she replied that, on the contrary, they had solidified and she was now a confirmed agnostic. She was very relieved when the rabbi reassured her that:

> To be a good Jew, you don't have to believe in God…just do what God says.

Not all would have such an inclusive attitude, but it reflects an acceptance that many Jews are no longer believers but are still committed to Jewish life. Whereas before, few rabbis would have bothered asking about belief, and many congregants would not have answered honestly, now there is awareness of the discrepancy between faith and identity and a willingness not to let it become a test of Jewish authenticity.

Of course, the fact that some Jews no longer accept the existence of God but still remain within the Jewish orbit poses a challenge for rabbis. Judaism is based on a deity. As former Chief Rabbi, Joseph Hertz, declared: 'Judaism stands or falls with its belief in the historic actuality in the Revelation at Sinai.'[1] He did not regard himself as being controversial, but just stating the obvious. The core activity of synagogues is still worship. Although many other activities may be organised – educational, social, cultural, welfare – and even if they are better attended, it is the Sabbath services that form the main function of a congregation. Even those members who never attend them would feel it a gross failure if they were to cease. It is as if it provides a stable centre, from which one can stray safely, and without its existence, Jewish life would dissipate irrevocably. The services also cater for those who do have a strong sense of God and derive an enormous sense of joy, comfort, solace, meaning, camaraderie and identity from them. Many rabbis will see those attendees as their key constituency and regard it as their duty to nurture them. The difficulty, therefore, is how to give two opposing messages simultaneously: affirm belief in God, but declare atheists are just as welcome. Equally, it is important not to let the dual message have a negative effect, and ensure it neither demoralises believers nor disenfranchises unbelievers. To adapt an image from the New Testament, we have to say loud and clear that the synagogue is a house with many doors, and it genuinely does not matter through which door you enter.

Not everyone will agree, and others will want to make distinctions and argue as to which is the main door, which the side door and which the tradesmen's entrance. However, it seems clear that if synagogues are to be places where all Jews can feel at home, then there must be plenty of open doors, all of which feel equally inviting.

---

1   Hertz, J.H., *The Pentateuch and Haftorahs* (1968, London: Soncino Press), p.402.

Adapting the prayer book

But some rabbis are willing to go further. Rather than just accept that some Jews will come to services and others will come to non-religious events, there is a remarkable attempt to bridge the divide and accommodate doubt within the services themselves. It first began in 1985 with the High Holy Day prayer book that was published for New Year and the Day of Atonement services by the Movement for Reform Judaism. Amid all the traditional liturgy, a passage was slipped in that recognised 'the God problem' that many were experiencing and spelt it out loud and clear:[2]

> *Perhaps God meets us and we do not recognise Him.*
> *He may speak to us in a chance remark we overhear,*
> *through a stray thought in our mind...*
> *[yet we have barred His access to us, so]*
> *He must steal into us like a thief in the night.*

It was a striking image that resonated with many, as did another prayer that acknowledged the difficulty:[3]

> *I confess that I let my knowledge of You fade away.*
> *Many hopes and visions died*
> *because I did not trust them,*
> *though they were the signs of Your presence in my life.*
> *I have stumbled through so many prayers today,*
> *and uttered so many words*
> *that I have lost touch with much of their meaning.*
> *I am bewildered by their certainties*
> *and their demands.*

---

2   *Forms of Prayer for Jewish Worship* (1985, London: Reform Synagogues of Great Britain), p.310.

3   Ibid., p.645.

It was an honesty that stood out from the blanket dec-
larations of faith and the affirmations of belief that
characterised the rest of the prayer book. This approach was
taken much further in the 2008 Daily and Sabbath Prayer
Book, which dedicated an entire section to supplementary 'Reflections'. The purpose was stated as 'to raise
some of the questions we bring to the prayers', though it
could have been even more explicit and instead said 'to
raise some of the problems we have about the prayers'.
It was based on the fact that: 'Many of the assumptions
[of the liturgy] belong to a very different understanding
of the world, the universe and God.'[4] In effect, it meant:
'We do not necessarily share the world view of those who
wrote the prayers, nor their understanding of God, and so
these passages may help us bridge the divide.' On the one
hand, this was an astonishingly brave admission; on the
other hand, the nervous language in which it was couched
showed how cautiously it had to be made, lest catering for
doubters offended the faithful.

The passages within the section continue the theme
of uncertainty and searching, with references to 'the
doubts, the confusion, the not knowing'. They also refer
to how: 'We may feel uplifted or distracted, bored or
inspired, moved or indifferent... We may leave this service
unaffected by its opportunities, having missed our way.'[5]
The readings do not offer answers, but the fact that they
express what many at services feel, or are unable to
articulate, or think they are unable to admit, allows them
to breathe religiously.

---

4   *Forms of Prayer* (2008, London: Movement for Reform Judaism),
     p.325.
5   Ibid., p.331.

That may solve many of the conundrums of an individual's belief, but it does not solve public affirmations, such as a *bar/bat mitzvah* (coming-of-age ceremony) for a young atheist or agnostic. To this, Alice's story offers a creative solution:

> Our second son, Ben, was a confirmed BuJew (another name for a Buddhist Jew). By the time it came to his *bar mitzvah*, in a stubborn but principled fashion, he refused to have anything to do with a traditional model that involved him saying things in public he didn't believe in private. Picture the scene in the rabbi's office: slightly despairing mother, somewhat truculent son and a beaming rabbi with an unexpected and inspired solution: Ben could read a blessing – one would be found that accorded with his principles – and give the sermon; his mother would read from the *Torah*, effectively having her own *bat mitzvah* alongside her son's *bar mitzvah*. On the day, rather to my amazement, the rabbi announced to the congregation that they were witnessing the synagogue's first atheist *bar mitzvah*. In all other respects it was traditional. The mother cried, the son gave a brilliant sermon on the moral difficulties and ambiguities of the story of Moses killing an Egyptian and the proud non-Jewish father read a passage from the Old Testament.

Ben is far from alone in his principled position. We dare any rabbi who disagrees with that assumption to ask a number of his or her members, aged 15–25 years, what they believe about God. The answer will provide a real challenge to traditional assumptions of Jewish theological conformity. Yet to us, like the new liturgy in the Reform prayer book, it is refreshing and empowering. We want to encourage the next generation to feel welcomed by a thinking and open-minded Judaism which offers them space to question, evaluate and change their mind – alongside a Judaism that is confident about the value of Jewish ritual and marking one's life cycle through time-honoured traditions.

This is a major step away from the attitude of 'Thou shalt believe', and even if it does not solve any of the question marks people bring with them, it does make those people feel like insiders rather than outsiders.

5

So You Think You're Jewish, Do You?

It should not matter if you only have one Jewish parent

I'm Jewish – are you?

What makes someone a Jew? As rabbis, we are often approached by people wishing to discuss their Jewish status. Some of those we meet may have documentary proof that they are a 'half' or a 'quarter', or even a 'sixteenth' Jewish; some will have uncovered their Jewish ancestry via a DNA test; some, in their quest to have a Jewish child via surrogacy, will go to extraordinary lengths to ensure that either the egg or the sperm donor is Jewish; some will self-identify as Jewish based on how they feel in their hearts – yet none of these post-modern ways of claiming and re-claiming identity can offer a sure-fire guarantee of recognised Jewish status.

It is never easy to have to inform someone that their understood Jewish status is not compatible with membership of a synagogue. As Joshua recalled:

I grew up thinking I was Jewish. I even attended synagogue with my father every single Sabbath. Yet when it came to booking my *bar mitzvah*, the synagogue would not allow me to have the same ceremony as all the other boys in my class. It was so unfair that I was excluded, just because I had the 'wrong' parent who was Jewish. If it had been the other way around and my mother was the Jew, then nothing would have been a problem. How is it fair that I was punished for something I had no control over? To this day I still feel Jewish, but they (my father's Orthodox synagogue) will never accept me.

For as long as there have been Jews, there have been those attempting to define who is and who is not considered Jewish. Whether it was a biblical census that recorded only the men aged between twenty and sixty who were fit for military conscription, or the numbering of the exiles returning with Ezra the Scribe, or defining who has the Right to Return when emigrating to the modern State of Israel, the process of definition provides a litmus test for both Jewish inclusivity and Jewish boundaries. In our pursuit of creating a welcoming and inclusive Judaism, we sometimes run into obstacles.

Of course, there is nothing wrong with boundaries – boundaries help us to make sense of the world; to know the difference between right and wrong, friend and foe, fact and fiction. The *havdalah* ceremony at the end of each Sabbath emphasises this importance of boundaries, not least through the final benediction:

Blessed are you, Eternal, our God, Ruler of the universe, who makes a distinction between the holy and the secular, between light and darkness, between Israel and the other nations, between the seventh day and the six working days. Blessed are you, Eternal, our God, who makes a distinction between the profound and the mundane.

Indeed, boundaries are, on the whole, a good thing, but what happens when these boundaries are so rigid that they hurt more people than they protect? Joshua's story is far from unique. Charlotte had a similar experience:

> I went to Israel on a summer programme with a Jewish youth movement. It was a wonderful experience and I loved connecting with my Jewish roots and my relatives who live over there. During the trip we visited Jerusalem and were given a chance to pray at the Western Wall. As I was walking towards the Wall another girl in the group grabbed my arm and told me that it would be disrespectful for me to join the others in praying because I wasn't properly Jewish. I fought back the tears at her cruelty. My mother is a Christian, but my brother and I have always followed the faith of our Jewish father. My brother is even circumcised. Who was she to tell me that I wasn't a Jew? It's taken me twenty years to get over my upset and come and talk to a rabbi.

As rabbis, we have encountered hundreds of people like Joshua and Charlotte. We hear their stories, feel their pain and want to help. For us, that is where Reform Judaism's unique approach should be best suited to traversing the boundary lines – striving to bridge tradition and modernity. Yet, this desire to combine historic Jewish principles with contemporary understandings of justice can create tension. Never is this tension more evident than in the question of who is and is not a Jew. Before we explain how Reform Judaism has found a way to help people like Joshua and Charlotte, let us first delve into the past and see how Jewish status was formed.

So, who is a Jew?

In early biblical times it was quite simple, you were Jewish if your father was Jewish. Joseph, Moses, King David and King Solomon all married non-Jewish women. Unquestionably, their offspring were recognised as Jews without any recorded process of conversion for either the children or their mothers. Ruth – who is often seen as the first convert – never goes through a formal, recorded process of conversion. In fact, it could be argued that her great-grandson, none other than King David, was only Jewish because Boaz, his great-grandfather, as well as Obed his grandfather, and Jesse his father, were all Israelites. Throughout the period of the Bible, Jewish status remained patrilineal (coming through one's father); this matched the patriarchal nature of Judaism. So, in the world of the Hebrew Bible, there were only two entry points into Judaism, either having a Jewish father, or converting.

This started to change in the fifth century BCE, when Ezra led the Israelites from Babylonian exile. On returning to the Holy Land, Ezra reprimanded the male returnees for their non-Jewish wives and their offspring of 'questionable' status. From that point onwards, Judaism ceased to be exclusively patrilineal, although it probably took some time for this to be formally recorded as the law. Very few Jewish legal records have survived from the period between the Five Books of Moses and the redaction of the Mishnah. The Mishnah is a rabbinic commentary on the

Bible, compiled by Rabbi Judah the Prince in the third century CE. It is the next major Jewish text after the Bible, which is why the Mishnah records Jewish law over the 800-year period that preceded it, including the rise and fall of the Second Temple. It is not clear exactly when the views of Ezra became the rules of rabbinic Judaism, but by the second century CE, Jewish status had become matrilineal. To paraphrase the Mishnah Kiddushin 3:12:

1. In the case of the child of a Jewish man and Jewish woman, where the relationship is not one of the forbidden unions (e.g. a priest marrying a divorcee), the child is Jewish and follows the father's line. **In plain English, that means Jewish father + Jewish mother = Jewish child.**

2. In the case of the child of a Jewish man and a non-Jewish woman, the child follows the 'lesser status' of the woman and is not Jewish. **So, Jewish father + non-Jewish mother = non-Jewish child.**

3. In the case of the child of a non-Jewish man and a Jewish woman, the child is Jewish but there is a stigma (this stigma is repeated elsewhere in the Mishnah; however, it is important to know that later on in their talmudic debate on the Mishnah, the rabbis removed this stigma, claiming that the child of such a union is an ordinary Jew and follows the status of the mother). **So, non-Jewish father + Jewish mother = Jewish child.**

Thus a major transition occurred, shifting Jewish identity to the mother if the father was not Jewish. But what motivated the very first rabbis to change Jewish status from patrilineal to matrilineal?

Jewish status vs. Jewish identity

Before we answer that question, let us dwell, for just a few moments, on the realities of today. In any Orthodox synagogue throughout the world, echoed by the official definition of the State of Israel, you are only Jewish if your mother is Jewish. It is that black and white; anything else requires conversion. Yet there is a difference between *Jewish status* (I am Jewish) and *Jewish identity* (I feel I am Jewish) – two rather different matters. One is how Jewish institutions classify you, the other is how you regard yourself.

To this day, in Orthodox Judaism, Jewish status is determined by one's mother, but certain aspects of Jewish identity, in keeping with the days of the Bible, continue to follow the patrilineal and patriarchal practice of early Judaism. In other words, if your father's Jewish identity includes the fact that he is a *cohen* (descended from the family of priests), then you are a *cohen*. However, if your mother is a *cohen*, but your father is not, then, like your father, you are not a *cohen*. Likewise, if your mother is Ashkenazi (descended from the Jews of Western European) and your father is Sephardi (descended from the Jews of the Iberian Peninsula), then you would define your Jewish identity as Sephardi and follow the Sephardi customs, even if they clashed with the customs and practices of your maternal grandparents. In fact, upon her marriage to your father, your mother would have adopted his Sephardi practices, forgoing her roots. As Sylvia writes:

> At first, it was strange to start cooking the dishes of my mother-in-law, especially at Passover when I had never been allowed to eat some of the dishes forbidden in my Ashkenazi household, including rice. When I went to synagogue with my husband, I didn't recognise some of

the prayers and the tunes were all different, although I loved the Mediterranean sound. It took me some years to feel comfortable in such a different environment, but by the time our son had his *bar mitzvah*, I felt like any other proud Sephardi mother.

Of course, this can get quite confusing, not least in modern times, when we all construct our identities based on the shared stories and customs of our parents. For these reasons, Reform Judaism has rejected the idea that Jewish identity can only be passed to us by our fathers, instead, we encourage every Jew to construct an identity based on reclaiming the rich tapestry of their roots, as well as being shaped by their life experiences and travels. As Sa'ar explains:

My father is Ashkenazi, my mother comes from Morocco, my three surviving grandparents live in Israel and I am working in the UK, dating a Jew whose family come from India. If you were sitting in my home, or eating in my kitchen, then you would see signs of all these cultures. I love being a Jew and I love feeling connected to so many places around the Jewish world.

Yet, whilst Reform Judaism has had no problem actively encouraging personal autonomy around Jewish identity and cultural association, when it came to Jewish status our boundaries were pretty inflexible.

Matrilineal vs. patrilineal

The reasons for that first great change – from patrilineal to matrilineal – have been lost to history. Perhaps, it was the influence of Roman law, which also changed in that direction. Perhaps, because of the commonplace rape of Jewish women during Roman times, one could only be sure of the mother's identity. Frustratingly, we have no records that explain the transition. All that is certain is that from the second century CE until modern times, Jewish status has been matrilineal. Gemma explains this quite simply:

> My mother is Jewish, even though my father is not. My mother's parents are both Jewish and were married by an Orthodox rabbi just after World War 2. My mother's, mother's, mother's, mother has been Jewish for as far back as I can trace my family tree.

Gemma's trouble is that her fiancé's father is Jewish but his mother is not, which creates a curious anomaly:

> Jeremy has three Jewish grandparents – his dad's parents are Jewish and his mum's father is Jewish. He's three-quarters Jewish, while I'm only half Jewish. But it's the one-quarter of Jeremy that really mattered when we went to an Orthodox rabbi and asked him to marry us. He refused, because I was Jewish and Jeremy was not. We were devastated but then stormed out when he suggested that we split up so that Jeremy could spend many years converting to Judaism. This has created so much upset for both sides of our family.

Until a few years ago, a UK Reform rabbi would have been faced with similar problems to an Orthodox rabbi. They might have been more sympathetic and tried to help pastorally but would have been equally constrained by Jewish law and unable to marry them. Gemma would be Jewish and welcome to join the community, but Jeremy would not. No Reform rabbi would have encouraged Jeremy and Gemma to split up, but they might have offered some alternative solutions, including Jeremy converting, or helping him to focus on the positive fact that his children with Gemma would automatically be Jewish on account of her matrilineal Jewish status.

Modern life has added further complications. Jack and Rudi had made careful plans for fathering a Jewish child through surrogacy:

> We found a Jewish egg donor who could prove her Jewish status – she even showed us her parents' *ketubbah* (marriage contract). We knew that we were both 'halakhically' Jewish and so we could guarantee that our child would have 100% Jewish DNA. We found a lovely woman in India who agreed to be our surrogate. When our son was born we were over the moon.

When Jack and Rudi approached their rabbi to discuss all this, they were shocked and greatly upset that their careful efforts to father a Jewish child had been in vain. It was left to the rabbi to explain that Jewish law does not determine the status of a child by the Jewish lineage of the egg donor (a concept which would have been unknown to the rabbis of the Mishnah nearly two thousand years ago) but by the womb from which the child was born. Jack and Rudi were devastated. They left their Reform synagogue and joined a Liberal congregation.

Since the 1950s Liberal Judaism in the UK has recognised anyone with one Jewish parent as Jewish, provided that there is a commitment to living a Jewish life. This approach, based on a deep belief in ethics and social justice, has enabled Liberal synagogues to welcome Jews with either a Jewish mother or father. Paul belonged to a Liberal synagogue for many years:

> I am a fourth-generation Liberal Jew. Both my grand-parents on my father's side were Jewish, but my mother came from a Christian family and, although she raised us as Jews, she never converted. I had a *bar mitzvah* in a Liberal synagogue. I went to Jewish summer camps every year and went on the national Israel tour when I was sixteen. When I fell in love with Jessica, we wanted to get married in her synagogue. Jessica's family are all Jewish and they've welcomed me with open arms. Unfortunately, her rabbi was not able to help, explaining that as I was not 'halakhically' Jewish, i.e. didn't have a Jewish mother, I would need to convert. I was disgusted at this rejection. Jessica and I went back to my Liberal synagogue and were married by my rabbi. Our future children do not need to be raised anywhere other than in a community that will not discriminate against them.

Like Liberal Judaism, since 1983 the American Union of Reform Judaism, the world's largest Jewish movement, has recognised both patrilineal and matrilineal descent. With both Liberal Judaism in the UK, and Reform Judaism in the USA accepting patrilineal Jews, the Reform Movement in the UK differed from its two closest sister movements. But tectonic plates were turning, and many Reform rabbis were exercised by the negative impact that rules from the past were having on individuals today. As one rabbi explained:

At the beginning of the summer, one of my last services involved marking the *bar mitzvah* of a patrilineal Jew in America. Then, I changed jobs and relocated to the UK. At the end of the summer, I found myself rejecting a prospective member because of his father's Judaism. It felt horrible and unjust.

Facing up to the challenge

In a Reform Movement that champions equality, it felt discriminatory not to include people because of the gender of their parents. Having resisted every previous opportunity to re-open the question of inherited status, a Reform rabbinic working party was established in 2013. The aim was to address the growing need to revisit and possibly revise the Reform position.

After a lengthy process, the working party identified one overarching principle – compassion: that children should not be punished for the status inconsistencies of their parents. This was backed up by the Talmud (Yevamot 47a), which offers an example of a man who converts to Judaism in a questionable way:

> There was a man who came before Rabbi Yehudah and said to him, 'I converted without witnesses or a rabbinic court.' Rabbi Yehudah said to him, 'Do you have witnesses to that effect?' He replied: 'No.' Rabbi Yehudah asked him, 'Do you have children?' He replied: 'Yes.' Rabbi Yehudah ruled: 'Your testimony would be reliable enough to disqualify your status, but it is not reliable to disqualify your children.'

From this principle we understood that if someone raises their children as Jewish, and the children assume that they are Jewish, even if the status of the parent later comes into question, the children are not held responsible and their status cannot be reversed. This is the same as a rabbi who was found to have been behaving in ways that are not compatible with the rabbinate. If the rabbi is removed from office, even if mistakes are uncovered from the past, the status decisions of the rabbi are not reversed. Just imagine if every wedding the rabbi had officiated at was suddenly deemed to be null and void. Likewise, if all those whose Jewish status documents the rabbi had signed and witnessed were then invalidated because the rabbi's signature on the paperwork did not count. Not only would this present a bureaucratic nightmare, but it would cause untold distress, sometimes across several generations. The rabbis of the Talmud were wise, in this case, not to visit the mistakes of the parents on their children.

Applying this principle to Kevin was not difficult:

> I had been raised as a Jew and it was only when I came to get married that I asked to see my parents' *ketubbah*. At that moment my parents sat me down and confessed that they had never been married under the auspices of a synagogue because my mother's mother was not Jewish, even though her father was. The rabbi who married them had only performed a religious blessing, not a civil one, and had created a *ketubbah* that would not have any standing. I don't know how my parents had been able to join a synagogue and to raise me as a Jew, but suddenly my world fell apart. Everything I thought I knew about myself came into question – who was I? How could I be anything other than Jewish?

How should Kevin be treated? Adherence to strict law suggests he be rejected as Jewish and the wedding be postponed until he had undertaken a course of conversion to Judaism. In contrast, compassion suggests his lifelong Jewish identity was sufficient for the ceremony to proceed as planned. Which response would be more in keeping with Jewish values?

The path ahead

The working party settled on a compromise position based on the principles of compassion and equality. Even just a few years on, it has become clear that it was not so much a compromise as a radical leap forward.

It was agreed that where someone has no Jewish lineage, i.e. no Jewish parents, there is a requirement to convert in order to be given recognised Jewish status and join a Reform synagogue as a member. Conversion remains an option for anyone who desires it.

Conversely, someone who has two Jewish parents is automatically given full Jewish status and can join a Reform synagogue as a member. However, if they have had no formal Jewish education or life experience, then deepening their knowledge and engagement is strongly advised.

The key area of change is where someone has one Jewish parent, irrespective of the gender of the Jewish parent. For them, there is no longer a need to convert. That is because the gender of the Jewish parent is not the primary determining factor in defining status. Instead, there must be a process for claiming the person's Jewish status. By going through this process, the individual removes any uncertainty of status that can come from having to choose between the different backgrounds of their parents. Most importantly, when determining the process, someone who has led a Jewish life, including in their upbringing and in their formal education, will be treated differently to someone who has not. The process may be a matter of days, months or longer – as tailored to the individual's experience and needs. To help with this decision the working party proposed eight areas that could be discussed with the individual as demonstrations of Jewish life in the home and synagogue:

1. Jewish home life past and present.

2. Attendance at synagogue past and present.

3. Knowledge of Judaism, including the festivals, life cycle and commandments.

4. Having lived aspects of the Jewish life cycle, for example *bar/bat mitzvah*, baby blessing, circumcision, a wedding blessing or mourning rituals.

5. Ability to read Hebrew.

6. Familiarity with the Jewish world and Jewish culture, for example, having visited or lived in Israel.

7. Formal Jewish education via Religion School, Jewish day school or in-depth adult education programme.

8. Involvement in the wider Jewish community, including charitable and humanitarian activities.

Accordingly, the length of the study course would vary depending on the person's knowledge and Jewish experience. Depending on the needs of the individual, they could appear before the *Beit Din* in person or simply have their paperwork sent for ratification. Likewise, they could, if so desired, visit a *mikveh* (ritual bath) as a way of physically marking their new status.

It was also decided that this new process was to include various opt-outs so that it could not to be automatically imposed on any rabbi or synagogue. Instead, any rabbi or synagogue who opted out would be supported in their initial position.

The response to the working party's proposal was significant. Over 80% of Reform rabbis endorsed the paper, a landslide. Many rabbis and synagogues immediately invited patrilineal Jews to meetings. Tara was thrilled:

> I never believed this day would come. At long last I will be able to join a Reform synagogue and not feel like I am under any suspicion.

The strong expectation is that, within the near future, all Reform synagogues and rabbis will embrace this new position.

What a difference

With many Reform congregations and rabbis keen to implement this substantial change in direction, a new three-stage process was introduced for helping an individual with one Jewish parent to claim his or her heritage and status.

Stage one involves an individual meeting with a rabbi to discuss Jewish status and life experience. The second stage is to agree, if necessary, a course of study and Jewish enrichment. The final stage is for the individual to sign a declaration of their commitment to return to their Jewish roots.

For any Reform rabbi working through the stages, it becomes quite obvious that every individual is unique and has made their own special journey back to their Jewish roots. As Ollie explained:

> I just wanted to be able to put all the years of uncertainty to bed. At long last I was as Jewish as all my friends who had one or two Jewish parents. The irony was not lost on me that, my whole life, I had been living a Jewish ritual life which was far more observant than many of my friends who had a Jewish mother but took their Judaism for granted. As soon as the *Beit Din* had signed my certificate, I went to the *mikveh*, held a private ceremony of welcome in my synagogue and booked my adult *bar mitzvah* to make up for lost time. I've never looked back.

Of course, not every case is as straightforward as Ollie's. Sometimes our compassion has to hit a boundary. Felicity, a young widow, came to see her rabbi:

> Having been married to a Jewish man for two years, I had been living a Jewish life with him. My grandfather was Jewish but my father was an avowed atheist. I was raised to be aware of my Jewish roots but had no formal education and we didn't practise any Judaism at home.

Felicity had Jewish lineage and some recent Jewish life experience. To deepen her Jewish knowledge and experiences, she was advised to embark on a year of study alongside synagogue attendance. However, upon closer analysis of her family documents, it became clear that

Felicity's grandfather had not been raised as a Jew, even though her grandfather's mother was clearly Jewish. After some debate, it was felt that the distance of three generations since Felicity's actively Jewish paternal great-grandmother was a little too far back to make a meaningful connection. Felicity was advised to convert, which she did with great enthusiasm. At her conversion, she appeared before the rabbinic court and was given both a Certificate of Conversion and a Certificate of Recognition, thereby acknowledging her distant Jewish ancestry. For Felicity:

> It was a profoundly meaningful journey back to my roots. I light my *Shabbat* [Sabbath] candles each week and think of my great-grandmother. I am so lucky to have found a synagogue and a community where I feel so at home.

In Felicity's case, conversion was the optimal solution, but for Daniel, it was a different story:

> I was raised as a Jew but was always aware that my mother was not Jewish. Growing up outside of London and having the 'wrong' Jewish parent came with lots of prejudice. I attended an Orthodox synagogue with my father but was not allowed to have a *bar mitzvah*. To compensate, my father took me to Israel and I had an amazing experience marking my becoming *bar mitzvah* just after my thirteenth birthday. Later on, at university, I was active in the Jewish Society. Eventually, I fell in love with a Jewish woman and we wanted to get married. A new system was in place whereby I was able to discuss my Jewish ancestry and my life experience with a rabbi. We filled in an initial form and it became clear that I had lived a very full and active

> Jewish life. The rabbi was able to promptly complete my
> paperwork and I was welcomed into my new community
> with open arms. I know that my children will grow up in a
> congregation where they will never experience any of the
> prejudice that I had to suffer. If I had met my wife just a
> few years earlier, none of this would have been possible.

All of this has created a very positive outcome for many
people who have previously felt shunned by Reform
Judaism. Yet, not every person needing to affirm their
Jewish status is an adult.

The next generation

Sometimes, there are couples who have young children, or
a baby on the way, and want some help. Their main reason
for approaching us is that one parent is Jewish and the
other is not. Their sincere desire is to raise a Jewish family.
The option of conversion for the non-Jewish spouse has
already been ruled out, but both parents are squarely in
agreement to raise their children as Jews.

In the majority of these cases we meet a Jewish father
and non-Jewish mother, based on the likelihood that a
matrilineal Jew will have found a congregation that recognises her children as Jewish, but this is not always the
case. Alison was shocked to discover that it could matter
about the difference between the gender of parents:

> I wasn't raised as a Jew, because my parents weren't
> remotely religious, and they wanted me to grow up without
> any fear or guilt. I knew that my maternal grandmother was
> Jewish and that her family had escaped Austria before the

Holocaust. Apparently, to keep their parents happy, my grandparents were married by an Orthodox rabbi, but that was about the last time Judaism mattered in their lives.

When I was in my early thirties, I met Abigail. It was a strange twist of fate that she was Jewish, as I'd never set out to meet a Jewish woman. Once we'd been together for a while, I became more involved with her family and started to reconnect to my roots. We decided to have a child and when I was pregnant, I went to the rabbi and asked her if I needed to convert for our child to be Jewish. She explained that because I was technically Jewish, I did not need to convert, and our baby would be Jewish. That didn't make sense, because another lesbian couple were in a similar boat but just because my friend's father was Jewish, rather than her mother, she had to convert. I don't think that is fair.

Irrespective of the gender of the Jewish parent, the process for affirming the Jewish status of a minor is similar to that of an adult. The one real difference is that, for adults, the process must take into account previous life experience, whereas for minors, it is about the commitment by the parents to give the child a Jewish future. Of course, there are various ways to assess this commitment, not least the Jewish knowledge and experiences of both parents, especially the non-Jewish mother. However, rather than waiting for any agreed parental Jewish education courses to be completed, time is of the essence. For a child, it is important to start Jewish life experiences as early as possible. Accordingly, when the rabbi interviews the parents, the rabbi's priority is to welcome the family and make them feel at home in the synagogue. Depending on the age of the child, attending Religion School or family services should commence immediately.

Francesca and Jamie had several children aged four to eleven. They had approached a Reform synagogue to explore whether there were any possibilities for enrolling their patrilineal children on the *bar* and *bat mitzvah* programme. As Jamie explains:

> We hadn't expected it to be so simple. The rabbi met with us, listened to our story, explained the paperwork that needed to be filled in and then invited the children to come back on Sunday to have a look at the Religion School. In that one meeting my children went from being Jew-ish, to Jewish, minus a few bits of paperwork. When I left the synagogue, I rang my parents and they cried down the phone. It was such a positive meeting that Francesca was only too glad to sign up to some Jewish parenting classes, and when our eldest marked becoming *bat mitzvah* I think Francesca must have been the proudest non-Jewish mother in history.

When Michael and Izabella came to see a rabbi they were surprised at how straightforward the process was to complete:

> Izabella had attended conversion classes, but all along we kept discussing that she wasn't ready to give up her Christianity. At the same time, she had no problem raising our future children as Jews. We completed the conversion course, but Izabella never went to the *Beit Din*. When our first daughter was born, we went to meet with our rabbi and he walked us through the new process. A few months later, on the day that our baby was issued with a Certificate

of Status, I took her into the *mikveh* and we both emerged as Jews. The following weekend she had a baby naming in front of the whole community.

At a time of unprecedented Jewish inter-marriage, when so many people are leaving Judaism, partly because it appears to exclude them, it cannot be overstated how important it is to retain the next generation of Jewish families. It is all well and good for Reform Judaism in the UK to have created such a welcoming policy, especially for young families, but until this policy is more widely known, there will be greater numbers of patrilineal Jews leaving than feeling that not only can they stay, but that they are wanted and welcome. It has taken two thousand years to embrace patrilineal Judaism once again, albeit alongside matrilineal Judaism. That rabbinic shift, almost two thousand years ago was, at least in part, to ensure the continuity of Judaism. With the UK's Reform rabbinate having taken a similarly brave and thoughtful step, now is the time to confidently share this radical, but all-too-necessary decision with the wider Jewish community.

Adoption

There remains one final issue of Jewish status that has not been addressed: that of the status of a child adopted by a Jewish family. Unless the birth mother was Jewish and there are status documents that can confirm her Jewish lineage, the child will not automatically be Jewish. Clearly, neither matrilineal nor patrilineal descent applies. The question is what can be done to welcome these children, especially at the end of what will have been a long and complex process of adoption for the parents?

As with all status cases, we try to make this as simple and straightforward a process as possible, without comprising any integrity. As Rabbi Jackie Tabick, the Convenor of the Reform *Beit Din* explains:

> There have been many occasions in the past when adopted children, brought up as part of a Jewish family involved in the community, think themselves to be Jewish, only to find out when they wish to celebrate *bar* or *bat mitzvah* or to marry in a synagogue that they first have to convert to Judaism. This can be a terrible shock. It is much better to sort out this issue when the person is young and it is relatively simple.

Following the legal adoption of a child, the parents sit with a rabbi and complete the appropriate forms. For young boys, circumcision is discussed but, as with all those seeking to convert a child, circumcision is recommended only for boys under six months of age. Once all the paperwork has been submitted, an appointment will be made with the rabbinic court. The parents will be interviewed by a panel of three rabbis and asked to sign a document promising to raise the child as a Jew. The rabbi is likely to have supplied some evidence of the family's commitment; for example, if the child is old enough, he or she may be attending Religion School or participating in children's services.

The appearance in front of the rabbinic court is designed to be a warm and positive stage at the end of what will have been a long and challenging process of adoption. Once the paperwork has been signed, a Certificate of Conversion is issued. The final step involves the child and the parents immersing in the ritual bath. Some time later, many parents decide to hold a ceremony of welcome in their home congregation, at which point their child is given his or her Hebrew name.

Lisa's story offers a great example of how she and her husband found the process:

My husband and I were both brought up in the Reform Movement. When we decided to get married in 1999, we became members of a vibrant, Orthodox community. Lawrence and I had always wanted children, but it was evident after a number of IVF cycles that this was not an option for us. With the support of Norwood we started our journey towards being a family and looking at adopting. We were blessed to be the proud parents of twins, Eva and Alex, whom we brought home from Russia in May 2010. We knew that we wanted to bring them up in the Jewish faith and we then looked into converting them.

As we were married under Orthodox auspices, we decided to explore the options of converting the children under their auspices. Unfortunately, we were faced with a brick wall and were told that if we wanted our children to be recognised as Jewish, we would need to become strictly observant and to undertake classes ourselves. This would have meant a radical change to our lives, values and beliefs, and, for me, I felt very strongly that we would not be true to ourselves. We were not good enough for the United Synagogue and nor were our children. Maybe we were naïve, we were warned to expect such a response, but it was the first time that as a Jew I had felt discriminated against. However, it made us more convinced that being members of the Reform Movement was right for us. We and our children have never been judged at any time.

Since we brought the children home, the synagogue has been there every step of the way, providing support with their conversion, with Alex's circumcision, the rabbi even coming to our house to put up a *mezuzah* [scroll with religious text] on the doorframe of the children's bedroom and another rabbi blessing us when Lawrence, Alex and Eva were in the *mikveh*. This support culminated in the most wonderful baby blessing in synagogue in July 2011 when the four of us were surrounded by our extended family, a memory I will cherish forever and feel emotional about to this day. As I reflect on the journey that my husband and I embarked on to fulfil our dream to have a family, we could not have achieved it without the love and support of our family and friends and also the rabbis at our local Reform synagogue.

You're welcome

From all of the personal stories and policies listed, there is no disputing that Jewish status can be rather complex. In our lifetimes, the Jewish world has changed, almost beyond recognition. Too often, the policies and politics of status have been placed before people. This can lead to the great pain and suffering of being made to feel like an outsider. There is nothing wrong with boundaries, but the questions that must always be asked are: 'Who are we trying to keep in?' and 'Who might we be keeping out?'

Our mission is to create a welcoming Judaism. It is future-facing policies like the UK Reform's new approach to welcoming patrilineal Jews that could make all the difference. Instead of families leaving Judaism, let us welcome them in, thereby strengthening Jewish households and congregations for years to come.

6

'I Never Knew I Was Jewish' Jews

The astonishing number of people discovering that they are Jewish

Family secrets

Joan was in her fifties and had lived in her village in Suffolk for over twenty years and was well known locally. She was a regular in the Women's Institute, was often seen at the village hall organising an event and went to church once a month. Her attendance there was more social than religious: 'being part of the community' was how she described it. She never considered herself a great believer, but enjoyed the hymns and found the sermons worthwhile. It was still a great shock, though, when her mother lay dying and told Joan that she had something important to say to her, which she had never revealed before: that she herself had been born Jewish and so, as Judaism was traditionally passed down through the mother's line, Joan was Jewish too. Joan was staggered. So many questions welled up:

> Why had my mother abandoned her Jewish origins? Why
> had she never told me? Why was she telling me now?
> What did she expect me to do with this new knowledge?
> What would my husband say? How would my children
> react? Were they technically Jewish too? Should I even
> tell them?

Joan's mother was too weak to go into great detail, but it seemed that she had been born into a Jewish family, but ran away from home when she was eighteen to marry Joan's father. He was not Jewish so, had she remained at home, her parents would have prevented the marriage from taking place. From their point of view, she had committed a 'double sin' – marrying without permission and marrying outside the faith – and she knew that they would have disowned her. In starting her new life, Joan's mother had decided that as she was leaving behind her family, she might as well leave behind her Judaism too, and neither she nor her husband ever mentioned her Jewish roots to anyone else. Whenever questions about her background had arisen, they were brushed away with: 'Oh that was a long time ago and too far back to remember!'

Joan, an only child, had been brought up nominally Church of England and had never had any contact with her Jewish family. However, Joan's mother had always been aware of her origins and, as her final moments approached, felt it important to keep the knowledge alive and pass on the heritage she herself had neglected but never forgotten. On hearing this news, Joan was not only taken aback, but also angry: partly, that her mother had kept from her such a significant part of Joan's own background. Partly that it was being revealed at a time when she could not react properly, as her mother's life was slipping away. However, she was not entirely surprised. She had always been interested in Judaism, although she had never pursued it beyond making a point of watching programmes of Jewish interest on television. She had also been conscious that she had felt drawn to the occasional Jewish people whom she had met over the years in a way that puzzled her:

> I remember talking to someone on a bus, and when she mentioned she was Jewish, I found myself warming to her immediately. That happened a number of times with others, which I thought was strange but never ascribed a reason to it. Now it suddenly made sense. They were not just Jews, but fellow Jews!

After her mother died and had the same Church of England funeral as Joan's father, Joan told her own husband about her mother's final words. To her relief, he was bemused rather than worried or horrified. He also agreed with her that they should tell their twenty-something-year-old children. They had never shared the Jewish affinity that Joan experienced, and simply saw the information as a factual detail in their family history. It was as if she had told them she had been born in Bournemouth rather than Brighton. When she mentioned that it meant that they could call themselves Jewish if they wanted, they felt that, while it was interesting to know, it had no relevance to them.

For Joan, though, it was the beginning of a journey, partly to delve into a past about which she had never known, and partly to discover 'who I really am today'.

When she told her husband of her intention to explore what it meant to be Jewish, he was entirely supportive. She decided to approach her local synagogue, but did not receive a positive response. Fortunately, she persevered and tried another one, and met with the rabbi. He confirmed that, although she had never practised a single Jewish observance in her life, she was technically Jewish and would be welcome to attend any services or other events. However, he did say that:

> It is not enough to have the label 'Jewish', you really need to know what it means for your own sake, otherwise it is meaningless.

He suggested she attend the 'Introduction to Judaism' course that the synagogue ran, covering the ABC of Judaism from an adult perspective. He also invited Joan's husband to come along:

> It's not that I want to convert you, but I think it's important you know what Joan's doing and feel at ease with her journey back to Judaism, even if it's not for you.

Joan's husband was happy to do so, and they also attended periodic services together. Joan felt she had 'arrived back home' and her church attendance stopped, although the rest of her life continued as before. As she explained to a group of her friends when discussing her experiences:

> I'm still the same me, but feel much more comfortable. It's not that I was dissatisfied in any way beforehand, but I suppose there were question marks about my mother's

background that I had got used to not knowing and never expected to find out, but now that I do know, I'm much more at one with myself.

The only issue that still bothers Joan is what would have happened if her mother had died suddenly from a heart attack or in a car accident. She would never have been able to pass on her decades-old secret, while Joan would be without any inkling of her Jewish lineage and probably still attending church:

I shudder to think how my life would have continued in ignorance – quite happily, I am sure, but unaware of my mother's past and without all the Jewish connections I now have. It's scary to think how that link might have been lost for ever.

Jason's experience was even more of a chance discovery. When his mother died, he and his brother, Julian, decided to sell the house she and their late father had been living in for almost fifty years. Given that each of them had fully furnished homes and they did not want to keep anything other than a few photographs, they were intending to get a house-clearing firm to empty the house for them. By coincidence, however, his boss reminded him that he still had a few days' leave that was due to him and he needed to 'take it or lose it'. The result was that Jason decided to use the time to do the job himself.

It was while he was emptying the loft that he came across an old suitcase that he could not open as the lock had rusted. He eventually had to force it open, upon which he discovered papers that astonished him. Several had strange writing on them, which he later found out was Hebrew, while there were cuttings from a paper called *The Jewish Chronicle*, as well as a marriage certificate indicating a wedding that had taken place in a synagogue. It was his parents' marriage certificate.

It was clear that Jason's parents had both been Jewish but had decided not to pursue it. More than just being lapsed Jews, they had consciously eradicated all reference to their religious background while Jason and Julian were growing up. It seemed that both parents had come to England from Germany at a young age, probably on the Kindertransport. Most of their mother's family had died in the Holocaust, while what remained of their father's family had gone to live in Canada.

When Jason and Julian started mulling over why they had been kept in the dark all their lives, they wondered if their parents had decided, in the light of their own terrible experiences under the Nazis, to try to shield their future children and grandchildren from possible recurrences of antisemitism. Jason also began to realise that disparate parts of his childhood now made more sense: the lack of an extended family, his parents never having any religious identity and their dislike of discussing anything to do with Israel in the news.

There was also the strange incident when he was eight and he used a word at home that he had heard at school – *mazeltov* – and the horrified reaction of his mother. She had told him off sharply, making him think at the time that it was a rude swearword, though he later learnt it was merely a Hebrew term for 'congratulations'. For his mother, though, it must have seemed a perilous moment, lest her young son was uncovering her concealed past.

For Jason, the discovery of the suitcase was a fascinating revelation:

> It had all the excitement of being on a treasure hunt...
> and with the added bonus that the prize at the end was
> me, or, rather, a fuller picture of me. For instance, I had
> seen several Holocaust films and found them interesting,
> whereas now they took on a new significance: they were
> not just history but autobiography.

Jason was fired up to learn both about Jewish history and Judaism itself. It led him to contact his nearest synagogue and enrol in a Basic Judaism class. This eventually resulted in him joining the synagogue, although his hectic business and family life precluded regular involvement:

> I don't have the time to go very often, but like to appear
> periodically and keep in touch. I felt it was important to
> reconnect with my history and this seemed the best way
> of doing that.

In complete contrast, Julian found the contents of the suitcase to be of purely academic interest, and it had no impact on his self-identity or lifestyle.

Perhaps the most intriguing aspect of Joan's and Jason's stories is that they are not unique. There are no records, but anecdotally there is clear evidence from rabbis in a wide range of congregations of people coming to them saying that they have just found out they are Jewish. In some cases, these people are in their twenties, other times they are much older. They may have been told by their parents, or been informed by other relatives, or discovered it by accident themselves. Sometimes it comes as a complete shock, whereas in other cases it answers a long-held suspicion that their life was not as it seemed.

For Connie, being told by an uncle that her mother was Jewish was not only a surprise but highly disconcerting. She was a practising Anglican and also a churchwarden. It led to a torrid period of religious questioning, with her wondering whether this affected her faith, and if so, whether it weakened it or strengthened it:

> In the end I decided that I was fortunate in that it made me part of the original tree trunk, not just a branch. It meant that not only was I a Christian, but I also had the same roots as Jesus himself. But until I reached that point, it was a rocky time religiously.

Conversely, Pat was delighted:

> I had always felt that there was something different about me. It was as if one of the pieces in the jigsaw of my life was missing. I had no idea what, but finding out I was of Jewish descent seemed to fill the gap.

The reasons for the mysterious cover-ups also varied greatly: in some instances, the parents or grandparent had simply been highly assimilated, so their Judaism lapsed into oblivion and the subject had never arisen. In other cases, it was a deliberate attempt to eradicate knowledge of the family's Jewish roots. This might be because it was felt burdensome in terms of social mobility or, as with Jason and Julian's parents, to protect the family from antisemitism. It could also be due to a Jewish person marrying someone non-Jewish and their roots quickly disappearing if their children were not brought up Jewish, leading to the grandchildren never even imagining they had a Jewish past.

Given that there has been a growing rate of inter-marriage since the 1950s, and that many families where both partners were Jewish have assimilated since their arrival in Britain, the number of people who have Jewish roots without realising it is probably very high.

Responding positively

From the Jewish community's perspective, the key question is how they should react to those rediscovering their Jewishness. Pat reported that when she approached her synagogue and asked if she could explore her Jewish origins, she was treated politely but told she would be better off going to her local library and reading books on Jewish life. When Joan enquired at her first synagogue, she was told that unless she had papers to prove she had a Jewish lineage they would not be able to help her. When she explained that, by dint of the situation, there was no proof, just her mother's death-bed confession, she was told that this was not sufficient and so it was not worth pursuing the matter. This is not only dismissive and hurtful on a personal level, but a major own-goal communally.

These individuals have Jewish roots, they are the products of Jewish history and they may well have been cast in the crematoria by the Nazis had they been living under their control. While many, like Julian, will not want to reconnect with Jewish life, those who are sufficiently motivated to knock on the door should have it opened.

Whether they are Jewish on their maternal or paternal side, whether it was their parents or great-grandparents who last had contact with Judaism, they should be greeted warmly. It is partly a matter of respecting their Jewish past and acknowledging that it gives them a claim to a Jewish present. It is also about the Jewish community reclaiming its lost numbers. No one will wish to rejoin unless they are sincere, so demands for proof should be mitigated where time, or the Holocaust, makes records impossible to obtain.

Rather than being seen as a nuisance or grounds for suspicion, the return of the rediscovered Jews should be viewed as an opportunity to redress past losses. An example of where a much more sensitive response was given was when Billy, who was brought up Jewish, found he was unable to prove his Jewish identity as his grandparents had been living in Austria and had deliberately erased all reference to their Jewishness to escape detection under Nazi rule. They had been highly successful in both endeavours.

Normally, the Reform *Beit Din* would insist on documentary evidence when asked to affirm someone's Jewish identity. In Billy's case, however, rather than reject his application, it was suggested that it would be acceptable to receive an affidavit from someone who knew his family and could assert they had been Jewish. The *Beit Din* took the view that even if the affidavit turned out to be dubious, it would be much worse to deny a Jew his identity. Better to be probably right than definitely wrong.

This principle was extended in the case of Orlando. On his thirteenth birthday his paternal grandmother presented him with a *kippah* (ritual head covering) and a Star of David and told him the following:

> Our ancestors were Jews who were forced to convert in Spain in the fifteenth century. If this hadn't happened, you would be celebrating your becoming *bar mitzvah* today. So, in honour of our ancestors, I am giving you these symbols of your Jewish heritage.

She also cited some examples of how his family had either kept certain 'Jewish customs', or had avoided incorporating too much into the religious community of the countries in which they had lived (Spain and Cuba). These customs included lighting candles on the Sabbath, keeping a vegetarian diet to avoid eating prohibited foods and maintaining a general ambivalence about religion to avoid becoming too involved with the Catholic community. One shocking detail she related was that she had personally circumcised Orlando's father in Cuba because there was nobody else that could do this for her. Orlando's parents had him circumcised medically a few days after his birth, and have insisted that all male grandchildren be circumcised as well.

Orlando is one of the growing number of *anusim* or 'Marranos' whose family kept not only kept their Jewish roots secret from the outside world, but maintained knowledge of it within the family for four centuries, and who now want to identify openly as Jewish. It is a massive step for them, but also presents a challenge of verification for the Jewish authorities. In cases where there is documentary evidence, then a Certificate of Return is granted by the Reform *Beit Din*; where this is absent, they join a conversion class so as to gain official status. In both instances, they are welcomed back. If they had been discovered in earlier centuries, they could have been subject to torture and even burnt at the stake, and for rabbis today to ignore four hundred years of Jewish identity would be churlish in the extreme.

Orlando himself has now joined a Reform synagogue and feels he has come home:

> We now regularly attend Sabbath services; we also maintain a progressive Jewish home, including the incorporation of our weekly observance of *Shabbat* and *havdalah*, our observance of the festivals and fasts. I like to believe that my formal return to Judaism has contributed something, however small, to the repairing of the damage caused to our people both by the forces that expelled us from Spain in 1492 and by those of our people who chose apostasy over exile.

Delving even earlier into Jewish history: in the year 722 BCE, ten of the twelve tribes of Israel were lost when they were transported away to the Assyrian Empire. From that date on, only two-twelfths of Jewry continued to be Jewish. Of those who survived, they faced a long list of local massacres over the centuries, or came through major attacks by the Crusades or Cossacks, only for a third to then be annihilated during the Holocaust. What remains today is therefore just one-ninth of the Jewish population that should have been in existence. Those who wish to become active members should be permitted to join in; those who wish just to learn about the past without being committed to current involvement should be helped; and those who are not sure what they want, but who wish to find out and explore the new situation in which they find themselves, should be enabled to do so.

All this will entail a personal welcome, and will require the rabbi to appreciate the emotional upheaval the individual may be experiencing. It also means that courses should be made available that provide a user-friendly guide to Judaism. In addition, there has to be sensitivity to the family dynamics, as the rediscovery may not be as thrilling for the person's partner or children, so it is important that it does not cause rifts with close relations. This would include tension with the person's parents if they were still alive, for they may be horrified that their careful attempts to put Jewish life behind them are now unravelling. But despite the need to avoid these potential problems, facilitating the return of Jews who have disappeared should be a considered a modern miracle.

7

The Women's Revolution

Ignored for far too long, women are at last achieving equality

If there have been several categories of people who faced unfair treatment in the Bible (see Chapters 2, 5 and 9), this was true of women as a whole. Throughout early Jewish history, including biblical times, there are records of individual women rising to positions of leadership, such as the judge Deborah. These were very rare and stand out against the overall trend of women being subordinate to men. The tone is set right at the very beginning when Eve is told by God that as punishment for her wrongdoing in the Garden of Eden, her husband shall rule over her (Genesis 3:16). This was taken as the template for all future male–female relations and was translated into religious life too.

It was only the men who were the religious leaders, be it priests in earlier times or rabbis after the first century. This did not stop particular women being recognised occasionally for their extraordinary qualities, such as devotion (for example, Hannah, the mother of Samuel) or great knowledge (including Beruriah in the Talmud), but they had no role within the institutional leadership. It has been suggested that men and women prayed together in certain parts of the Temple, but most scholars think there were separate areas; certainly, it became the norm in synagogue life for them to sit in different sections. Even this was not deemed sufficiently distinct, and it was ruled that women should be out of the sight of men, resulting in their being segregated at the back of the synagogue, sent upstairs or hidden behind a veil. For Alexandra:

> Growing up in an Orthodox synagogue, as soon as I was ten I was sent upstairs. I soon became aware that the service was only for the men. We women were out of sight, but rarely out of sound for we were so disempowered and disinterested that we talked about everything but the prayers and often were shushed from below. I can remember one particularly indecorous *Shabbat* morning when the rabbi told the women that they should neither be seen nor heard. That was the moment I became a feminist. I soon left Orthodoxy.

For centuries it had been ruled that men should not hear women during prayers, and so mixed-sex choirs were banned. By way of mitigation it was explained that this was necessary because men were considered to be spiritually weaker and therefore should not be distracted from their prayers by women. This was simply a justification for discrimination, and was such a blatantly weak argument that it was even more insulting.

Naturally, women could not also take part in any of the active roles in synagogue worship, such as opening the Ark or reading from the scrolls. The result was that women were second-class citizens in the synagogue, restricted in both access and participation. Of course, the discriminatory nature of this arrangement was always denied, and Orthodox authorities claimed that men and women merely occupied different roles: that whereas men were supreme in the synagogue, women were supreme in the home, and so everything balanced out. However, the oft-cited formula 'equal but different', when scrutinised, does not correspond to equality.

Given the assumption that husbands ruled their wives, that formula was a very dubious assertion, but either way, the overall statement was a tacit admission that women did not count in religious life. This was reinforced by the rule that a full service could only take place if there were ten adults present, but this referred only to men. Thus, in a room in which there were nine men and thirty women, it still lacked a quorum (*minyan*) of ten people. The thirty women were effectively invisible. Moreover, because of the gendered nature of the Hebrew language, if there were thirty women present and only one man, when addressing those present in Hebrew, the language in use would be masculine, because conventional Hebrew always priorities men over women, irrespective of when women are in the majority.

A consequence of all this was that women's Jewish education was largely ignored, for if they had no synagogue role, it was wrongly assumed there was little need for them to learn Hebrew or understand the structure of the service. This then became a self-perpetuating policy, with women feeling cut off from what occurred in the synagogue and men making all the decisions, thereby reigning unchallenged. It was only in the mid-nineteenth century that the downtrodden role of women began to be addressed. With hindsight, it is astonishing that it took so long, although it reflected the second-class role women occupied in most other faiths up to that point, as well as in public life in general. In politics, business, academia and most other fields, it was taken for granted that women had no right to be involved.

Empowering women

In 1840, the West London Synagogue of British Jews was the first Reform synagogue to be established in Britain. Its object was to respond to the needs of the time, in which Jews were no longer segregated in physical ghettos from mainstream society, nor in mental ghettos. The founders wanted a form of Judaism that corresponded to the religious and social changes around them. Although the twenty-four founders were all men, a new attitude to females was evident from the start. Henceforth the coming-of age-ceremony at thirteen years – at West London called 'confirmation' – was to be for both boys and girls. On those occasions, girls participated equally and read from the *Torah* scrolls and the Prophets. Women's voices were no longer deemed a distraction, and in 1858 a mixed-gender choir was introduced.

The revolution had begun, although it continued at a cautious pace in other areas. Separate seating, for instance, was maintained, and it was not changed until the inter-war years, at which point, in 1933, women sat in the main part of the synagogue, together with men. With hindsight it is surprising that this was not one of the very first reforms, but it is taken for granted nowadays. Certainly mixed-seating is seen as one of the most defining characteristics of Reform Judaism by Orthodox Jews, as well as by those outside the faith. There may be plenty of theological and liturgical differences that can be regarded as highly significant, but the fact that men and women sit together is the most immediately striking aspect when one enters a Reform synagogue. Perhaps, in the early decades after the break with Orthodoxy, and with the flush of excitement at the other reforms that had been introduced, seating arrangements felt less of a pressing issue. Thus, the long-ingrained cultural assumption of men and women praying separately was harder to challenge than frustrations over the inordinate length of services or exasperation at prayers with content that was deemed inappropriate, such as animal sacrifices.

Today, however, the revolution is complete, and when a group of Reform teenagers was taken on a visit to an Orthodox synagogue recently, so as to experience other forms of Judaism, there was an explosion of anger afterwards by the girls at having to sit upstairs, with the boys below. As Chloe said:

> It felt like we were animals at a zoo, caged away. Clearly, we didn't count, and weren't wanted. It was insulting beyond words. How on earth can the women there put up with that each week?

An obvious physical difference between men and women in services was that the former were obliged to wear a *kippah* and *tallit* (prayer shawl), whereas the latter were not. It was often stated by Reform rabbis that there was no objection to women doing so, but it was not until the mid-1970s that it was gradually taken up. Even now, however, it is still a minority of women who choose to wear them; though the numbers are increasing. Whereas women have been willing to overturn other previously exclusive male domains – from seating arrangements to leading prayers – the sartorial area was either considered a less important obstacle to overcome, or was too associated with cultural behaviour to be tackled. It may also be because it has been left as a personal decision and not institutionalised, so as not to force women to wear the *kippah* and *tallit* who did not wish to do so. The intention may have been to avoid discomfort, but the result was to make wearing them a proactive decision and to stand out from others. As with Janet's experience, this inadvertently raised the stakes and changed it from being a simple development to a life-changing moment:

> The thought of putting on a *tallit* in front of 'all those people' made me quake. What would they think I was…? Twenty possible accusations sprang to mind. Was I really just an exhibitionist after all? Did I want to be like the men in some way I could not yet understand? Was I a hypocrite to don a trapping of piety when I was in fact struggling with my own belief in God? Had my feminist consciousness found yet another barrier to smash through?

In Janet's case, eventually she 'summoned up the courage' to wear a *tallit* and, like many others who chose to do so, felt spiritually uplifted.

In other respects, too, there have been major advances, such as in the way the male bastions have fallen at all stages of the life-cycle rituals, from cradle to grave. The life of one particular woman, Geraldine, highlights the new Jewish world that has opened up for women in Reform circles:

In the Orthodox tradition, the arrival of a girl usually means that the father is honoured by being called up to the reading of the *Torah* the following week, with the mother and child being treated as if irrelevant, without any role and often not even present in the synagogue. However, when I was born, I was the centre of attention. I was taken to synagogue and given a blessing in front of the Ark, with both my parents actively taking part in the ceremony. At thirteen, I had a *bat mitzvah* that was exactly the same as my brother's *bar mitzvah*, leading the Sabbath morning service and reading from the scroll. Conversely, an Orthodox girlfriend was not allowed to read the scroll, and had a pleasant but limited ceremony on a Sunday that was separate from the main service.

When I got married, I had an equal role in the wedding service, exchanging a ring with my husband and saying the Hebrew formula that bound us together as a couple. When my Orthodox girlfriend got married, she did not do anything and was completely mute throughout her wedding. Some years later, when both of us lost a parent, I was treated as the main mourner and recited the memorial prayer, the *kaddish*, at the funeral. Being an Orthodox woman, my friend 'did not count', and so a male relative said the memorial prayer on her behalf. In all these instances, I did not feel that I was being given special privileges, but just doing what is normal for a Jewish person to do. I am not thankful that, as a woman I can post letters in the same letterbox as men, I take it for granted as normal behaviour. So too with my Jewish life.

As well as giving women equal access to Jewish rituals, various ceremonies have been created to respond to their particular needs. A miscarriage, and the loss of the hoped-for child, certainly affects men, but it is women who bear the physical effects and may suffer much more emotionally. Special prayers have now been composed to cater for the sense of loss, guilt and trauma that can be felt at such a time. One powerful composition declares:[1]

> *You were a collection of cells,*
> *but already my child, with a secret name*
> *and a secret voice.*
> *My hopes bled away in the night*
> *and I am left with the pain*
> *of where my baby used to be.*

Another prayer was for women facing a mastectomy:[2]

> *Now that I must begin a journey of damage and*
> *destruction, of pain and grief*
> *help me to keep faith with those who seek to cure me*
> *give me strength and courage, trust and hope*
> *cover me in the shelter of your wings*
> *hold me to Your breast and comfort me.*

While some such prayers were written by men, it is noticeable that the vast majority are composed by women. It is they who usually identify these needs and can address them best. It is also women who have designed special welcome ceremonies for daughters, known as *simhat bat*, which take place in the home shortly after birth.

---

1   Romain, J.A., *Really Useful Prayers* (2009, London: Movement for Reform Judaism), p.71.
2   Ibid., p.73.

It recognises that, for centuries, boys have had a formal moment of Jewish arrival via circumcision, but there has never been a mainstream equivalent for girls. So, women have created a new ritual that is infused with songs, poems and prayers, and that also recognises the physical and emotional experiences of the mother.

The effect of women rabbis

Perhaps the most dramatic breakthrough in terms of equality was the arrival of female rabbis in the UK. It had long been mooted as a possibility, but did not occur until 1975 when Jackie Tabick was ordained. It was not due to any change in attitude, but was more an occurrence-waiting-to-happen. She had approached the Leo Baeck College to study Judaism in greater depth. The Admissions Board decided that there could be no objection to a woman wanting to learn – others had done so in the past for twelve to eighteen months before dropping out to take up other careers – so the Admissions Board decided not to take a view as to what might happen if Jackie completed the course five years later. They would deal with this at the time if it ever arose. However, in Jackie's case, she did complete the course and passed all the exams, at which point it was decided that there was no serious reason not to ordain her, and so she was duly made a rabbi. They were well aware that many congregations would not wish to employ a female rabbi, but the College took the view that her future employment was a separate matter from the right to be a rabbi. In the event, she did gain a position immediately, and later went on to serve other communities.

Her emergence was enormously influential in two senses. First, it encouraged other women to come forward. Sybil – later a rabbi – was at university at the time studying theology and pondering her future career:

> I wanted to do something with a religious dimension to it. In those days, as a Reform Jewish woman, there was no chance of teaching RE in what were, then, only Orthodox Jewish schools. I opened the paper one day and saw a picture of Rabbi Jackie Tabick's ordination and thought: 'I can do that'.

Sybil's eureka moment was typical of many women who had previously thought that they could only enter the Jewish community via a side-door but were now able to come through the front. Back in 1967, Holocaust-escapee Rabbi Arieh Dorfler had delivered a withering indictment and passionate challenge:

> Progressive Judaism has failed pathetically in the last hundred years, both in having neglected the intensive education of women in Judaism...and in not having attracted them to the ministry as a spearhead in the drive to invigorate Judaism within and without the Jewish home. Let us open the gates now, and after the destruction of our great, learned European Jewry, strengthen our ranks by recruiting gifted Jewish women to the Institutes of higher learning.[3]

By 2019, just over fifty years after his dramatic plea, almost half of all rabbis serving Reform synagogues were female.

---

3   Dorfler, A. (1967) 'Open the Gates', *Living Judaism 1*, 3, p.81.

Second, there were also many women who did not want to pursue a rabbinic career, but did wish to be more empowered in synagogue life. Although Reform congregations all agreed about women's equality, there were still those who held back on certain involvements, such as reading from the scrolls. As Tammy put it:

> I felt able to challenge my community and say, 'Look, if we can have a female rabbi reading from the *Torah* every week in her synagogue, why can't I do so in mine every now and then?' And it worked.

The momentum created by a female rabbinate also led to innovative practices, especially in life-cycle events, such as thanksgiving rituals for the birth of a girl and prayers for those who had experienced a miscarriage or reached menopause. There were also monthly study sessions for women only, known as *Rosh Hodesh* groups. As one participant, Sandy, commented:

> It is a remarkable time to be a Jewish woman, for after years of neglect and dismissiveness, suddenly the floodgates have been opened to unleash a torrent of female creativity.

The female route to the rabbinate had been a very pragmatic approach that was in complete contrast to that of the Church of England, where a similar debate was swirling. However, the Church regarded the issue of female clergy as a theological question: whether or not it was in keeping with ecclesiastical precepts? Its protracted discussions and the fraught task of unifying those for and against gender equality in the ministry meant that women's progress was delayed for another two decades. The first female priest – Angela Berners-Wilson – was ordained in 1994. Although the position of Deacon had been open to women long beforehand and permitted them to lead many ceremonies, it did not allow the person to officiate at the most important ritual, the Eucharist, which only a male priest could do.

Within Orthodox Judaism, there was no question of women becoming rabbis, and the debate instead focused on whether or not they could be given access to talmudic and other studies that had been hitherto reserved for men. This was granted in certain 'middle-of-the road' institutions. On the positive side, this has resulted in more knowledgeable women, but – as opponents feared – it has also added to the pressure for them to be given greater roles in Jewish life.

While many Orthodox women are content to be schoolteachers, others wish to use their new-found knowledge in a rabbinic context. As a way of accommodating this, women are permitted to teach other women and lead women-only services, but not to teach men or to lead services at which men are present. Whilst this is regarded within Orthodoxy as responding positively to the new climate of women's rights, in reality this still imposes a religious glass ceiling on their talents. Yes, it may be extending the boundary a little, but it locks firmly in place the distinction between what women can and cannot do. The very first Orthodox woman in Britain to gain a form of ordination for women known as *rabba*, Dina Brawer in 2017, could only do so via a course in the United States. She then found she could not use her expertise here as fully as in the United States, and emigrated.

The language of prayer

The new climate within Reform Judaism led to a major change in the liturgy that corresponded with the appreciation of gender-inclusive language in wider society. Whereas masculine terminology had been seen previously as covering both males and females – such as 'All men shall praise the Lord' – it became increasingly viewed as archaic and non-representative. Exclusively male terms began to grate both on male and female ears and became seen as alienating. It was often noted that women made up 50% of the congregations, yet were being excluded from the prayer book. As Katie put it:

> I can't point to the exact moment my perceptions changed, but I do know that whereas prayers about 'every man' or 'all men' once included me, now they no longer do so. In fact, they push me away and make me feel that the prayers have no relevance to me. My conversations with other women suggest that this is a widespread problem.

A new edition of the Daily and Sabbath Prayer Book (*Forms of Prayer*) was therefore published by the Movement for Reform Judaism in 2008 employing gender-neutral language, with the above becoming 'All people shall praise God'. Similarly, 'our fathers' became 'our ancestors'. It was a small shift in wording, but a massive development in thinking, acknowledging that women were worshipping as women, not as add-ons to the men.

Moreover, new wording was inserted into the traditional texts, such as references to the Patriarchs being accompanied by mention of the Matriarchs. Thus, the central prayer, the *Amidah*, was changed to mention not only Abraham, Isaac and Jacob, but also Sarah, Rebecca,

Rachel and Leah. Women were no longer just inferred, but specifically named. Some objected that it disturbed the familiar flow of the prayers, but habit is not an answer to principle. Within a short space of time, regular use of the new liturgy soon made it become the new norm. As Monica, a warden in her synagogue, put it:

> Before long, we came to question when all the other Reform liturgies would be updated, e.g. the High Holy Day prayer book which now sounds so archaic without gender-neutral language.

The religious significance of language was also recognised with regard to God and to which descriptions were used. Masculine imagery was replaced by gender-neutral terms. Thus, God was no longer 'King' but 'Sovereign', and no longer referred to as 'Lord' or 'Master' but 'God'. It reflected a wider world in which hereditary monarchs with absolute power, usually male, have been replaced by female prime ministers who were democratically elected. It was also an attempt to educate congregants away from the idée fixe of an old man in the sky and substitute an image that was free of male-oriented preconceptions. Some newer liturgies occasionally describe God as 'She' – though many would regard that as being as unacceptable as 'He' – because several of the names of God are feminine, for example, the *Shekhinah*. Perhaps this is an attempt both to encourage free-thinking and to push the pendulum the other way so that it eventually settles somewhere in the middle and ends up with a God who is gender-free.

The steady advances of gender equality provoked opposition in various quarters. In some cases, objections came from men who felt their domain was being infringed, such as by women leading services; in other cases, it was from women who enjoyed their set role and did not want to be forced out of their comfort zone, especially when other women started wearing a prayer shawl. Sometimes the criticism was merely from individuals, other times whole congregations decided not to make any changes, such as not allowing women to read from the scrolls. In all these cases, though, the objections were largely based on emotion rather than reason, with objectors claiming that 'it doesn't feel right', instead of justifying their position with sound arguments. In such cases, the solution was the passage of time, by allowing people to become used to the new realities.

There was one congregation, for instance, which allowed girls to read from the *Torah* scrolls for their *bat mitzvah*, but not to do so afterwards, as 'women don't do that here'. They were caught between wanting girls to have the same Jewish skills as the boys, but not wanting to change the familiar pattern of their services. It was a position that was totally illogical and could not be sustained in the long term. Michaela, as she approached her *bat mitzvah*, remarked pointedly:

> I don't understand what all the fuss is about. I'm just as good as any boy and I want to keep reading Hebrew as a Jewish adult. Why can't I continue to lead the service? My first cousin is allowed to because of what's in his trousers, not what's in his head or his heart.

The waiting game often caused intense frustration amongst the women who wanted to see faster progress in their communities. One by one all the objections fell away in the face of common sense. As Philip, a self-confessed opponent who eventually put aside his resistance to full equality, explained:

> At first, I was led by my eyes – someone in skirts leading the service – shock! horror! But then my ears took over, and she was either inspiring or boring, engaged me or nonplussed me, just as the male service-leaders did.

The result is that, today, women in Reform synagogues are equal in all respects, occupying rabbinic roles and equally involved in all religious aspects. The same applies to communal organisation, with women being lay leaders and serving as chairs of synagogues. This is not to say that there are never any hiccups or awkward moments, for there are still those with misogynist attitudes, mirroring wider society. Women can still be treated in degrading or dismissive ways, sometimes by ordinary members and sometimes by those in a position of authority. It is important not to lose sight of that fact that the majority of discrimination comes from unpleasant individuals, rather than institutional bias. In that respect, the battle has been won and, unlike women in Orthodox synagogues, who still face many limitations to their rights of participation, the principle of female equality reigns supreme.

8

Falling in Love Across the Religious Divide

The growth of mixed-faith couples and how best to respond

The new social reality

In the 1960s and 1970s it was not uncommon to find rabbis giving sermons about the 'cancer' affecting Judaism. It was a particularly powerful image, in a time when cancer was becoming more and more feared, and before the period when medical treatment had found ways of ameliorating its impact, or even overcoming it. However, the 'cancer' to which the sermons referred was not a medical condition, but the growing number of Jews marrying non-Jewish partners. The rabbinic objections were a concern both that it would take the Jewish partners away from Judaism and that any children would be lost as well. The latter was even more important, because it would cut off an entire line. According to rabbinic law, the very first command given by God was 'to be fruitful and multiply' (Genesis 1:28). For Jews this meant passing on the faith to the next generation, echoing Deuteronomy 6:7, a verse that is the basis of what is often regarded as the most important Jewish prayer in the entire liturgy – the *Shema* – which is recited twice a day. Whereas some faiths are primarily about the individual and his or her salvation, Judaism is about continuity. It is very telling that a key definition of what it means to be a Jew is to have Jewish grandchildren. It is not enough to be a good Jew yourself, you have to guarantee the future of the community.

The intensity of the opposition to mixed-faith marriage was sufficiently powerful to even describe it as 'doing Hitler's work for him' – in other words, helping to destroy the Jewish people, who lost a third of all Jews worldwide in the Holocaust. Initially, this opposition was echoed by most members of the community, whether for these reasons or others. One was shame – that a son or daughter had breached the communal taboo. As Richard put it:

> For years I have been a stalwart in the synagogue and someone whom others respected, but after my son married out, I now feel everyone looks at me differently.

Another reason was a sense of guilt that they had not instilled a strong enough Jewish identity in their child to resist the charms of someone non-Jewish. It made Muriel question her own parenting skills:

> I look back and constantly ask myself, 'Where did I go wrong?' and feel I have failed as a Jewish mother.

For others, there was more a sense of worry that the religious divide would make the marriage less secure. Ken spoke for many when he said:

It's important for any couple to share as much in common as possible and certainly to want to bring the children up in the same way. The more they differ, the more the marriage is likely to come under strain.

But there was also a darker reason for opposing a mixed marriage that was epitomised by Valerie's forthright view:

The first time they have an argument, it'll come out [antisemitism] and he'll call her a 'bloody Jew' and it'll go downhill from there.

Curiously enough, the parents of the non-Jewish partners would sometimes be equally against the marriage, either because of their concern about its chances of success, or because of latent dislike of Jews. They might have Jewish friends, and genuinely get on well, but having Jewish in-laws was a step too far. There were also those who had no objections in principle and who liked their Jewish son/daughter-in-law personally, but were anxious about their grandchildren. As Mary remarked:

I saw what happened to the Jews in Hitler's Germany and I worry that, by marrying someone Jewish, my son is now putting his children on the front line, which wouldn't have been the case if he'd married someone ordinary.

Whatever the reasons for rabbis and parents opposing their marriage to a non-Jew, for those concerned it was a brutal shock to hear their deep love being labelled as 'a cancer'. It was equally shocking to be told they were acting as Hitler's surrogate. Danny – who was a member of an

Orthodox synagogue and had a non-Jewish wife – was at a service when the rabbi used such terminology in a sermon condemning mixed-faith marriage:

> I stood up and declared: 'I know exactly who you are talking about' and walked out.

Whether or not the rabbi was actually referring to Danny is a moot point, but he felt it was the case and never returned.

Most others did not take a public stand but either seethed in private or expressed their anger to friends. They did not see the situation in those terms at all. They saw no contradiction between valuing their Jewish identity and falling in love with someone non-Jewish. Whereas the rabbinate tended to regard 'marrying out' as 'opting out', they had no intention of abandoning their faith. In some cases, they had already mapped out with their partner how to lead a dual-faith household; in other cases, this was a discussion yet to be undertaken. Either way, they felt it was their community or their family who had rejected them; not them doing the rejection. When they eventually walked away from Jewish life, be it loudly or silently, it was with a deep sense of regret. As Malcolm said, wistfully:

> Loving Christine didn't make me feel any less Jewish, but I was made to feel I had to make a choice between the two of them. It wasn't so much that I chose her above Judaism, just that I never saw it as an either/or game and stayed with her, but that seemed to settle it for everyone else. If I was with her, then I wasn't with them. That wasn't how I saw it, but I took the hint and we went our own way.

The cost of love

The loss to British Jewry from mixed-faith marriage was enormous. No records were kept, but the size can be inferred from the synagogue marriage statistics, as synagogues can only perform weddings that are recognised by English law if both parties are Jewish, so mixed-faith weddings tended to be held at registry offices. The number of marriages that took place in synagogues in 1950 was exactly half that of 1930. During this period, the Jewish population had not decreased – on the contrary it had expanded due to 60,000 Jews who had arrived from Nazi Europe before 1939. The dramatic drop in synagogue marriages can be put down primarily to the sharp rise in mixed-faith marriages. It became 'public enemy number one', with rabbis declaring that although antisemitism was terrible, at least it bonded Jews together and reinforced their identity. Mixed-faith marriage, by contrast, peeled Jews away from their families and the community at large. It was, therefore, a much worse threat to the future of British Jewry.

This inevitably begs the question: were the rabbis right to be so aghast at mixed-faith marriage, or was it a major over-reaction on their part? They were potentially right for two reasons. First, for almost two thousand years, Jewish status was passed on through the mother's line (see Chapter 5). A person was Jewish the moment they emerged from a Jewish womb. It was an inherited status and not subject to any declaration of faith or initiation rite such as baptism. Boys would be circumcised eight days after birth, but they were already Jewish, and a lack of circumcision would not alter that fact. This meant that if a Jewish male married a non-Jewish female, their children would lack Jewish status in the eyes of the Jewish community, and so 50% of all mixed-faith marriages carried an automatic loss to the community. If the reverse happened, and a Jewish female married a non-Jewish male, their children automatically had Jewish status.

Second, if they were not brought up Jewish, then in real terms they too dropped off the Jewish radar. This might have occurred because the father was opposed to having them brought up as Jews, or because the mother was disinclined to do so if she felt rejected by the community, or because the simplest way to avoid conflict in a dual-faith household was to make it a religion-free zone and not bring up the children in either faith. Sally was far from alone in repeating the parental mantra:

> We're not giving them one particular faith, but will let them decide for themselves when they're older.

That may have been wise in terms of domestic diplomacy, but it meant that, not having been brought up in any faith, the children often chose to remain that way and contributed to the rising number of 'nones' that have come to characterise British life. Thus, even though many of those children technically had Jewish status, realistically it did not count in terms of Jewish continuity. So whether it was a Jewish male or female who 'married out' of the community, the odds against their children remaining Jewish were high.

Another problem arose even when the mother was Jewish. Her Jewish status meant that her children were deemed Jewish. For many of these women, their non-

Jewish husbands were entirely supportive of the family carrying on the Jewish tradition. Yet in some cases, synagogue Religion Schools were unwilling to allow these children to attend, or reluctantly did so but made the mother feel so disapproved of that she did not want to participate, let alone expose her children to a hostile environment. As Helen explained:

> Even though the synagogue knew full well that I was married and had changed my surname, they still insisted on sending me the monthly newsletter to my maiden name addressed as 'Miss'. After a while I decided that if they couldn't accept that I was married, it was not the place for me or my children.

Even when synagogues were more accommodating, it could be difficult creating a meaningful Jewish home life when the father did not join in. Carole spoke for many when she said:

> For me, like most of the contemporaries I grew up with, Jewish life came from the home. We talked Jewish, ate Jewish, did Jewish. It was automatic, and Judaism is very much a domestic faith. I wanted to re-create that for my children, but at the same time I didn't want to alienate Paul who had no experience of that sort of thing. I felt stuck in the middle and, in the end, gave up. We did go to my sister's for Passover every year, and Paul would always join us, which was great, but it meant that Judaism was outsourced and, from the kids' point of view, did not rub off on them.

Mixed what?

It should be noted that although the term 'mixed-faith marriage' is being used for a Jew who marries a non-Jew, it does not necessarily mean that the other person has a faith of their own. In fact, it is very rare that they are religiously observant in another faith, otherwise the differences might prove too large to bridge. In most cases they are lapsed Christians, with a vague attachment to Christian traditions (such as christenings and Christmas), but not strong believers or regular worshippers. In a surprisingly high percentage of cases (26%) they come from the Catholic tradition.[1] This is doubly strange given that, first, Catholics and Jews have a more tumultuous, blood-filled past history compared with Jews and Anglicans; and, second, that there are relatively few Catholics in the UK to meet and fall in love with in the first place.

Part of the mutual attraction may be because both are minorities in Britain, and have suffered discrimination, so they share a certain world view. It is also easier for two minorities to marry – as neither feels they are 'selling out' to the majority culture and can better appreciate each other's distinctiveness. In addition, although Judaism and Catholicism have considerable theological differences, lapsed Jews and lapsed Catholics are not bothered by them. Instead, they share the core values of both faiths, such as personal ethics and family life, which make them comfortable with each other.

There are also many non-Jewish partners who have no faith at all. In some instances, this makes life easier for the couple as there is no conflict of interest, and the

---

1   Romain, J.A., *Till Faith Us Do Part* (1996, London: Fount), p.156.

non-Jewish partner is happy to go along with a moderate amount of home ritual ceremonies and sees no objection to the children having a Jewish education if that is important to their partner. In other cases, though, the non-Jewish partner is opposed to any form of religion, with the result that the children are not brought up as Jewish. It also means that the Jewish partner is unable to express their own Jewishness – if not religiously, then culturally – and has to suppress those longings or risk conflict within the marriage.

In recent years, a new variation has arisen: Jews who marry Muslims. This was an inevitable development as the Muslim community in Britain became increasingly integrated and those who were second or third generation followed the same social patterns of wider society. In some ways, Jewish–Muslim marriages are much easier, as Rachel (married to Mo) explained:

> We never have any of the difficulties that some of my Jewish friends married to Christians have, such as over not having pork in the house, or the really big one about circumcising male children. It's a given for both of us.

However, there can be problems when announcing the relationship to parents and grandparents, with some Jews regarding all Muslims as potential suicide bombers and some Muslims regarding all Jews as gun-toting right-wing settlers. It can be fraught enough introducing potential in-laws to each other at the best of times, but much worse when both sides want to dive for cover.

Someone who had been married twice and could measure the differences was Margaret, who was wed to a non-Jew for many years and, some years after his death, went on to marry someone Jewish. She expressed the situation that she and many others had experienced when she said:

> They were both good marriages, but the latter was so much easier in terms of religious culture. It was the difference between getting into a cold bath and a warm bath. With my Jewish husband, I just slipped in and immediately felt comfortable without having to work at it.

It reminds that alongside the difficulties there were also many cases of mixed-faith marriages succeeding. The factors that attracted the couples to each other in the first place lasted through the marriage. Despite the cries of woe and predictions of doom from rabbis and family, the divorce rate for mixed-faith couples has been only marginally higher than for same-faith couples.[2] As for the children, although some end up as a religious battleground, many we interviewed found that they benefited from a dual heritage and felt at home in two traditions. The children only felt confused if there was conflict between the parents. As Layla (aged ten) put it when discussing her mixed-faith parents:

> Of course, parents are different: Mummy and Daddy are a different shape and different size, they have different smells and do different things, so why shouldn't they be different faiths too?

---

2   Ibid., p.143ff.

The terrible sin in some people's eyes is a perfectly natural situation for others.

It should also be emphasised that mixed-faith marriage is not a phenomenon that has affected just the Jewish community in Britain. Catholics have an even higher out-marriage rate, while faith communities that are newer to the country, such as Muslims, Sikhs and Hindus, have also begun to experience it. The factors are the same: first, young adults marrying later in life and often leaving their parents' home when still single. They are thereby more independent of parental influence, while their primary influences may come from their social circle. Second, people moving away for jobs and therefore settling in areas that are removed from their birth community. Third, the more secular nature of society, which views equality and inclusivity as important values that often override religious loyalties. Fourth, the unintended consequence of the growth of interfaith dialogue. It has not only lessened hostility between the faiths but has brought home the fact that, as is often put colloquially 'we are all the same underneath', thereby weakening resistance to social relationships across the religious divide. The number of those from minority faiths who have married members of the Church of England, whether active or lapsed, has increased to such an extent that in 1992 the Church commissioned a special Order of Service as guidance for priests officiating at weddings for dual-heritage couples.

Jewish responses

The picture above indicates that British Jewry is standing at a crossroads. Mixed-faith marriage is a sociological reality, with the latest estimates suggesting that 26% of Jews take a non-Jewish partner.[3] It is the result of trends that the Jewish community cannot control and that operate within society at large. The wishful thinking that a few trenchant sermons could solve the problem has proved to be misplaced. The next step also failed: a rush to build Jewish day schools, which, it was hoped, would at least give the rising generation a stronger Jewish identity and thereby prevent out-marriage. The problem was that although their pupils were certainly enclosed in the Jewish world until they were 18, these young Jews still then emerged into the surrounding culture, be it at university or work. It was there that they met non-Jews and fell in love. Often, it was unintended, in that they had envisaged marrying someone Jewish, but, as Darren explained:

> Up to that point, all my girlfriends were Jewish, but it just so happened that at the office I met Pam, and that was that.

Jewish day schools may have given their pupils a better Jewish education and stronger identity, but they did not stop them falling in love with non-Jews after school age.

Two radically different routes became open to the Jewish leadership. The first was to highlight the difficult personal experiences of out-marriage, hunker down, become more inward looking and try to raise the drawbridge between Jewish life and the outside world as much as possible. The second was to recognise that mixed-faith marriage is an

---

3   Graham, D., *Jews in Couples: Marriage, Intermarriage, Cohabitation and Divorce in Britain* (2016, London: Jewish Policy Research).

inevitable part of an open, pluralist society, will continue to be so and British Jewry has to come to terms with it. In a revolutionary move, this latter path was adopted by Reform rabbis. The objectors were right to be concerned about mixed-faith marriage, but that does not mean they responded in the right way. In fact, there are many reasons to be positive, particularly bearing in mind two aspects that have already been mentioned. One is that many of the non-Jewish partners did not have a strong faith, or even any faith. In some cases they were Christians who adhered to the ethical teachings of the Church but did not believe in Jesus; others had never been brought up with a faith, but were not averse to it. In these instances, many of them would be happy to adopt Judaism, either because they valued it themselves or because they felt it important to have a unified household.

Judaism is not a missionary faith, out to 'grab souls'. It holds that there are many paths to heaven and it does not matter which one a person takes. As far back as the first century, the rabbis declared that: 'the righteous of all nations have a place in the world to come' (Tosefta Sanhedrin 13:2). However, if people wish to convert and come of their own accord, then conversion is possible. This will be examined in more depth (see Chapter 11), but for now it is sufficient to report that a negative mind-set towards converts developed after talmudic times, largely because of the social gulf between Jews and non-Jews caused by centuries of persecution, expulsions, ghettos, blood libels and inquisitions. Even in the modern era, the default position has been to turn applicants away, partly because of the fear that they may not be as observant as the rabbis want, partly because it is seen as 'a backdoor to mixed-faith marriage' and effectively endorsing it, and partly out of suspicion of anyone not from a Jewish blood-line. The latter is a form of racism, of which the Jewish community should be ashamed.

It is surely time to change the negative attitude towards conversion. Applicants should be greeted with a smile rather than a scowl. A conversion request should be seen as a compliment to Judaism, not a threat. It will also have a dramatic effect on the impact of mixed-faith marriages. The Jewish partner will be bringing a new person into the community. Instead of losing Jews, it will be doubling the numbers! Even if the non-Jew is not fully observant and is converting more for domestic harmony than for their personal spirituality, they will at least ensure that their partner remains in the community, thus keeping Jews Jewish.

There will also be many non-Jews who do not feel it is right to convert, perhaps because of a latent attachment to their own faith, or because they do not want to upset their family, or because they lack any faith and feel it is hypocritical to become Jewish. However, they may still feel that the values associated with faith are beneficial for their children, while they might also regard the home rituals as important for family dynamics. In these situations, the person may not want to convert, but would be happy for the children either to formally acquire Jewish status or to be brought up in a Jewish environment and identity, even if their status is not fixed. Unfortunately, the Jewish community is obsessed with status and is not comfortable with children being indeterminate. Many Sunday morning Religion Schools, even within Reform synagogues, will not allow a child who lacks Jewish status to attend despite the fact that one parent is Jewish and both parents favour their participation.

This, too, needs to change. Jewish education should not be withheld from children with a Jewish heritage. Synagogues must be flexible enough to value children from Jewish lineage being within their midst, without fussing over paperwork. Even if status is still held as important, it should not prevent education. It is also a matter of getting used to 'playing the long game', so that even if the children are not 'officially' Jewish and their parents have no intention of making changes, let them have the Jewish experiences that might lead to them taking up Judaism in adulthood and passing it on to their own children.

The other aspect of the existing situation that makes this new, more welcoming approach so very appropriate is the attitude of the Jewish partners. Most feel very positively about their Jewish roots and have a strong Jewish identity. For some, this comes from their early home life, for others it arose as a result of attending a Jewish day school. Most would endorse the comment of Frank that:

> I never intended marrying out, but it just so happened that way. What's more – and I know this may sound silly given the choice I've made – I'd still like my children to marry someone Jewish.

It means that many Jews who marry non-Jews still want to be part of Jewish life, still want to be involved in the community and still want to pass on the Jewish heritage to their children. In the past, we have shown them the door and locked it shut behind them, whereas if we now not only leave it open, but also walk them through it, they will be only too pleased to regain their Jewish home. Mixed-faith marriage, therefore, may give plenty of challenges to the Jewish community, but it also presents many opportunities. It is like those who look at a rose bush and see the thorns, whereas others focus on the petals.

For far too long, we have let fear and suspicion be our guides, whereas it is now time to be welcoming and constructive. It is still appropriate to say that we prefer Jews marrying Jews – for religious and cultural reasons – but it is equally appropriate to say that those who do not find a Jewish spouse remain just as Jewish as before, and their partners can be as Jewishly involved as they wish to be. We cannot legislate for whom Jews fall in love with, but we can make sure that both they and their partners stay within the Jewish orbit. As Alice reminds us:

> I have many reasons to be grateful to Reform Judaism, and particularly to our synagogue. I was ringing around various local synagogues to see whether they would be right for my young family, and especially my non-Jewish husband. Almost all the conversations went like this:
>
> Me (apprehensively): 'Hello. I'm a lapsed and out-of-practice Jew, looking for a synagogue to join. My husband is not Jewish. Is that a problem?'
>
> Synagogue staff member (in warm and welcoming tones): 'Of course it's not a problem.' And then there would be a pause, after which the synagogue staff member would venture the following question: 'And when will he be converting?' Clearly it was a problem.
>
> By the time I rang our local Reform synagogue, I was expecting the same question. But it never came. Which

was something of a relief. Everybody has their own way of managing an interfaith marriage, and I would no more have asked my husband to convert than he would have asked me to get married in a church. We've been members ever since.

Making love succeed

It is symptomatic of the deep well of myopia into which British Jewry has fallen, that Jewish readers may consider this open-door proposal to be highly daring, whereas readers outside the Jewish faith may be puzzled that it was not adopted long ago. This myopia is partly historic because of the inward-looking nature of the Jewish community, caused by the terrible experiences in Christian Europe in both medieval and modern times. It is also born of a fear by the current leadership that if it opens the door too wide, the community might be swamped by wider society and lose its identity. However, the worry about giving the green light to assimilation ignores the fact that mixed-faith marriage and assimilation is already happening of its own accord. If secular culture can be depicted as a deep river flowing past both sides of the tiny island of British Jewry in its midst, then it certainly needs to have signs up saying 'Danger. Beware of the strong current' to prevent people from falling in. But it is equally necessary to offer swimming classes for those who want to enjoy the waters without being swept away, as well as having a supply of inflatable lifebelts for those who find themselves in difficulty.

It should be axiomatic, therefore, that when a member of the community calls the rabbi to say they have become engaged to someone non-Jewish, the rabbi should not slam the phone down, as still happens, but arrange to meet them. At the meeting itself, it may be the case that the rabbi points out the pitfalls that the couple may encounter, but as a matter of information, not as a precursor to suggesting they break off the relationship. It should also be the case that various options are discussed, such as the non-Jewish partner converting to Judaism, or not converting but attending an Introduction to Judaism class, so as to gain some understanding of the culture and family into which they are marrying. It should also be expected that the Jewish partner attends these classes too, both to be supportive of their partner and because they themselves might benefit from refreshing their Jewish knowledge and plugging any gaps. Many Jews finished their Jewish education at thirteen years old and as a result have the religious knowledge of a spotty teenager, so it is a chance to upgrade their Jewish understanding. A religious quid pro quo should also occur with the reverse taking place, so that the Jewish partner learns about their partner's religious background and traditions. The respect has to be mutual and, like the marriage itself, religious tolerance has to work for both partners equally.

The families of both partners have a key role to play too. It could be that they have reservations about the relationship, and they are perfectly entitled to express doubts respectfully ('I don't think he/she will be willing to go along with what you want') or ask questions ('Are you sure you are both heading in the same direction?'). However, these should be done constructively and without rancour or abuse. There should also be a cut-off point. Once the couple is engaged, the relationship should be accepted and celebrated. If not, then the parents may well jeopardise having meaningful contact with the couple or any input into their future. The Jewish family should certainly use this period – if they had not started earlier – to introduce the non-Jewish partner to Jewish home ceremonies, such as a Sabbath evening meal or the family *seder* at Passover. While this may seem obvious to some, as a way of combining both warmth and education, many Jewish families have resisted. Ginny expressed this on the grounds that 'it only encourages them and implies we approve'. Whilst these may be legitimate feelings, they are not a sensible strategy for building long-term harmony. Instead, by the time an engagement is publicly announced, the family needs to have accepted the choices that have been made and react as positively as possible. The same welcome and introduction to home life should be undertaken by the other family.

A radically new attitude should also be taken to the wedding day. There should be no question, as occurs in some families, of boycotting the wedding and staying away. It is a hurt that the couple will not forget. Even if relations improve over time, the parents will never be able to put themselves back in the half-empty wedding photographs. However much they may feel despair and however much families would have preferred a Jewish–Jewish wedding, relatives should go with good grace and suppress their desire to stand there with gritted teeth. Even more abhorrent are the more extreme cases of Jewish families sitting *shivah* when the marriage takes place. This is the ritual that takes place after a close relative has died. By adopting this for a living person, it implies that they are as if dead and will no longer be counted as part of the family. It is wrong on so many levels: it is a ghoulish rejection; it does not stop the wedding going ahead anyway; it closes off any chance of further contact; and it may not particularly help those sitting *shivah* as they know full well that their son/daughter is alive and may have children, their grandchildren, whom they will never meet.

Just look at the musical *Fiddler on the Roof*. Tevye's daughter, Chava, 'marries out' and her parents sit *shivah*, a living death. But how many people know what happens at the end of the original story upon which it was based, Sholom Aleichem's *Tevye the Dairyman*? Chava finally returns home. Here is what unfolds:[4]

> Out of the other room she came, my daughter Chava, as unspoiled and beautiful as ever – a little more careworn perhaps, a little less bright-eyed, but with her head held high, like a queen. For a minute she just stared at me, the same as I did at her. Then she held out her hands, though all she could say was a single whispered word: 'Pa-pa'... What [else] should [I,] Tevye have done? Taken her in my arms, hugged her and kissed her, and told her...come to me, you're my own flesh and blood.

In complete contrast to the great pain of a family break-down, the wedding should be seen by family and clergy as a wonderful opportunity to marry not only two people, but two traditions. The ceremony should reflect aspects of the heritage that both partners bring into the marriage. The only caveat should be that no reading or ritual should be included that might cause offence. Many Jews, for

---

4   Aleichem, S., *Tevye the Dairyman and the Railroad Stories*, translated from the 1916 original by Hillel Halkin (1987, New York: Schocken), p.129.

instance, would not object to the name Jesus, but might find references to 'Our Lord and Saviour' difficult. Balance, compromise and sensitivity need to reign supreme. The role of clergy from both sides is crucial. It starts with that phone call asking to meet. Alternatively, if the rabbi hears about it through someone else, they should take the initiative, contact the couple, congratulate them on the engagement and offer to meet to discuss the issues ahead. Some might consider this colluding with the act of 'out-marriage,' or even prostituting oneself, but it should be seen as a pastoral duty, not to mention civilised behaviour. After all, in a troubled world, the joy of two people finding love is something to celebrate.

After the wedding

The meeting with the rabbi would itself certainly look at the wedding ceremony and discuss creative options. However, far more important than the four or five hours of the wedding are the next forty or fifty years of the marriage. It will be vital to discuss topics that the couple may not have talked about. For instance, what will go in the fridge: Only *kosher* food? Only non-meat? Anything? Even if the couple do not care, will it be wise to have pork chops on display when the family comes around? There is not necessarily one right answer, but the couple must find the answer that is right for them. One couple, Seth (lapsed Jewish) and Kate (lapsed Church of England), married thirty years ago. Here is what Kate recalls:

> We never had any divergence over food as Seth often ate pork or lobster at restaurants back when we were courting.

However, when we had our first weekend back in our new home following our honeymoon, I decided to treat him to breakfast in bed and brought up bacon and eggs. He went ballistic and I was both hurt and shocked. Seth had simply never explained that he did not eat pork products in the home, just outside. To me, this made no sense at all, although many Jews will recognise the distinction, however, illogical. It was a pertinent lesson in not making assumptions about each other, about what we each did and did not do religiously, and about how much we understood about the other, even after two years together.

Another good question is what religious images will be present in the home? Either partner may wish some symbol – be it a crucifix, Buddha, *mezuzah* – and the other person has to be comfortable with it, as well as having the ability to put up their own icon if they so wish. It also means the right to say: 'No, I do not feel comfortable with that in the house' and deciding that, to avoid conflict, the home is a religion neutral zone. This may be particularly important in December as newly wed Leona (nominal Christian) found out when she brought home a small Christmas tree that she thought would make a lively decoration for the front living room, but which Harry (Jewish) saw as a declaration of religious war:

It took us months to get past it. I'd never lit a *hanukkiah* [nine-branched candelabrum] before in my home, but that year I made sure to light it every one of the eight nights. I sat in one room with my *hanukkiah* and left Leona alone with her Christmas tree. It felt colder inside than the December weather outside. Our marriage almost didn't survive that winter. Of course, the following year we worked out a happy compromise, but it involved a lot of heartache to get there – something we could have avoided with a frank conversation when we first met.

The children

One of the biggest topics in the discussion will be the children. Couples can happily work out compromises between the two of them – such as she goes to church on a Sunday, while he goes to a car boot sale and they meet up for lunch afterwards – but when a third party is involved, it becomes far more complicated. On a simple level, the questions are: Which parent does the child go with, or does he/she alternate activities? Do both parents feel equally comfortable with that arrangement? On a more complex level – but which is core to the discussion – the rabbi should help them separate the 'what are we going to do with the children' question into three component parts: religious education (what a child knows), religious status (how others see the child) and religious identity (how the child views itself).

In this framework, a range of options are possible, including identity in one faith but knowledge of both, or dual identity with dual education. In Pam and Frank's case, they wanted to bring their son up Jewish like his father but to feel comfortable with both sides of his family. It meant that he had Jewish identity, non-Jewish status and dual education. Gerry and Sandra took a different route:

We brought our son up Jewish like his dad, and our daughter up Quaker like her mum. While some might wonder at our splitting our children, for us it proved to be a harmonious solution and our children were not fazed by it.

It is when parents are squabbling, or silently resentful, that the children suffer religious confusion. It highlights the fact that what works best is the scenario that fits each particular couple. The discussion is complicated by the fact that it is not simply a matter of logic, but is clouded by emotion. Very often, those who evinced no strong religious feelings when single or married, suddenly discover deep subterranean religious feelings when they become a parent. Traditions they never seemed to care about suddenly become important. This can be a genuine shock to them, but even more so to their partner, who had thought they were marrying someone lapsed or secular. As Alasdair explains:

> It is perfectly natural to fondly remember the feel of one's childhood home and the smells coming from the kitchen. This leads many to want to re-create them for one's newborn child, but it can be a problem if there are different, or even conflicting, memories from those of one's partner's upbringing. That is when raising a child can become an unexpected tug-of-war.

This applies even more so with initiation rites: if the couple has a baby boy, do they circumcise him, or baptise him, or do neither, or do both? The issue is particularly acute as circumcision usually takes place eight days after birth, so one has to make fairly quick decisions about them. It is vital that the couple have discussed the matter well in advance and are not forced into a hasty decision when they are exhausted physically and overwhelmed emotionally.

A topic that also needs to be tackled – although it is frequently ignored by those concentrating on the wedding day – is what will happen in the event of a death. The usual questions about whether a person wishes to be buried or cremated, and where, are more complex for a mixed-faith couple. If they wish to be buried together, then many Jewish cemeteries only permit Jews to be interred and therefore they might have to opt for a non-denominational cemetery. It means that many mixed-faith couples choose to have a cremation – with their ashes scattered under the same rose-bush – but it may not be what they initially desired. There is also the issue of who should take the service: the minister of the partner who died, who can give the correct last rites, or the minister of the partner who survived, who can give the traditional comfort?

Here, too, there is an urgent need for change by the Jewish authorities. Jewish cemeteries should be less restrictive, and certainly when it comes to allowing the burial of partners of Jews. Why should a couple who have been together for several decades be separated into different cemeteries in death? If it is a punishment for having married out of the faith, then it is extraordinarily petty at a time when compassion is most needed. If it is to protect dead Jewish bodies from the 'taint' of non-Jewish ones, that is a terrible example of post-mortem racism. It is also harsh on the children who are forced to visit their mother and father in separate places, rather than side by side in the same location. The couples may need to plan ahead, but the rabbinic authorities also need to re-evaluate their policies.

This has now happened in Reform cemeteries in recent years. Some have created special sections for mixed-faith couples within the overall area; others permit them to be buried in the main section. Like so many innovations, it seemed a radical step at the time, but, with hindsight, seems an obvious development and totally in line with Jewish values of assisting the dead and comforting the bereaved. Moreover, the anticipated explosion of objections never materialised. On the contrary, the move was greeted with relief. As Mandy expressed it:

> Being a mixed-faith couple has not meant any frictions in our marriage, and so far we have had thirty-seven wonderful years together. However, as the years go by, I have wondered what will happen when the end comes, and I had begun to dread the thought of being in different places, rather than being side by side. It is such a comforting image. When I discussed it with my rabbi and he said: 'You have been together in life, so the same should apply in death', I burst into tears. I hadn't realised it meant so much to me, and that it had been like a dark cloud hovering in the back of my mind.

Bless you

If all of the above should be part of the pre-marriage discussion with a rabbi, then it is also important that the rabbi accompanies the couple throughout their ongoing religious journey and, if they so wish, this may well include the rabbi being part of their wedding ceremony. As mentioned above, synagogues are only empowered by British law to marry 'two people, both professing the Jewish faith'. So, for their wedding to be legally recognised, the vast majority of mixed-faith couples opt for a registry office ceremony, but this still leaves open the possibility of having a blessing in synagogue afterwards. In the past, rabbis have refused to officiate, echoing the centuries of shunning mixed-faith couples. For some rabbis, this refusal may have conflicted with their inner feelings, especially when the people asking were relatives or close family friends. For other rabbis, the idea of participating was out of the question. The more extreme said that it was a sin, which they could not condone; the more progressive declared that, although they are happy to be involved in the rest of the couple's life, they could not participate in the act of out-marriage itself. The latter point may seem reasonable to the rabbis, but feels like a rejection to the couples.

Here is another revolution: in 2012 many rabbis decided that if they wished to keep the Jewish partner involved in Jewish life and make the non-Jewish partner feel welcome, then they had to be with them on one of the most important days of their life. Reform rabbis will now offer a religious blessing after the legal ceremony. They might either lead a short service or be one of several people doing readings. It should not be underestimated both how radical and how effective this new development is. Reflecting on the blessing ceremony, Frank said:

> Judaism has always been part of who I am, and I wanted it to be something I carried into my marriage, so it was important to me that my rabbi was involved in the moment it started.

For Sophie (Jewish) and Tom (atheist, from a Church of England family), they wanted their wedding to reflect their future:

> We had long discussions with our rabbi and were delighted when we learned that we would be able to

have a wedding blessing in the synagogue after our civil wedding ceremony elsewhere. We both really liked the idea of being able to celebrate our marriage in a Jewish context that was meaningful and welcoming for both sets of families. The setting was also important as it had become the focus of our Jewish life during that period. Being able to have a Jewish ceremony was also great for Tom's relatives as an introduction to the Jewish family life we were hoping to nurture. We worked hard with our rabbi to create a ceremony in which everyone could take part, and feel involved. We were happy to be doing something that made us think deeply about the marriage we wanted to build together.

Of course, for some couples, there is a desire to represent both faiths on their wedding day equally. There are some rabbis who are willing to co-officiate with the minister of the non-Jewish partner. Whilst each rabbi will have his or her own rules about these things, and Reform Judaism offers some clear guidelines, most Reform rabbis who are unwilling to participate themselves will pass on the phone number of a colleague who is prepared to do so. There are also a small number of mixed-faith couples who hold the wedding in church if the non-Jewish partner is particularly involved there. It can present difficulties for some members of the Jewish family if the church is full of icons, and some may even boycott the ceremony, feeling it is a 'step too far'. The couple need to bear this in mind when choosing the venue, and also opt for a vicar who will understand the swirling sensitivities. Once again, though, families need to think long term and put aside reservations about the ceremony in favour of maintaining relationships with the current and future generations.

There are two golden rules in mixed-faith marriages. One is for the couple: discuss everything in advance, so that there are no unexpected hiccups or ongoing sores. The other is for rabbis: turning away a couple achieves nothing, whilst engaging with them means Jewish continuity. The rabbinic change in attitude has taken a long time to arrive, and in its absence countless couples have been lost to the Jewish community. Now, however, rabbis have begun to catch up with social realities, and they may be able to stem the outflow.

Non-Jews in synagogue life

The significant percentage of Jews who have married outside of the faith means that there are many non-Jews who are on the fringes of Jewish life. Some are happy to stay there, regarding Jewish involvement as their partner's private domain, as much as if they were football fans or antiques collectors, and nothing to do with them. Others, however, find they are drawn into synagogue life through their partner or their children. As Howard put it: 'Marrying Jeannie effectively meant marrying her community too, although I didn't realise it at the time!' He does not go to services – 'not my thing' – but like many other non-Jewish spouses, he attends periodic social events or takes the children to Religion School on a Sunday morning. All Reform synagogues welcome this engagement, with non-Jewish partners welcome at all activities.

However, it begs the question of to what extent non-Jewish family members can be involved more formally in synagogue life if they so wish. Here practice differs, but all within a positive spectrum. Some synagogues are happy for them to be on sub-committees, while others have schemes which enables them to formalise their status by becoming 'associate members' or 'friends of the community'. They can certainly participate in cycle of life ceremonies involving relatives, such as standing by their son or daughter when they read the *Torah* at their *bar/bat mitzvah*, or being under the *huppah* at a wedding. Some rabbis will also allow them to perform certain rituals in the service itself, such as opening the Ark or holding the scroll while it is being dressed, especially if it is during a special occasion for their family, such as a baby blessing or *bar/bat mitzvah*. There are synagogues that would not countenance this, but as one rabbi put it: 'We are so conditioned by the Jewish/non-Jewish divide of former decades, that we put up barriers when there is no need, and object to involvements that cause no harm. We have to educate ourselves out of such negative thinking'.

The same new approach applies to time of death. As discussed in Chapter 8, non-Jewish partners can be now buried in a Jewish cemetery, which was strictly forbidden in the past. In addition, the Jewish partner will be helped to observe the same mourning rituals as would be normal for the loss of a Jewish person, if that is what they wish. This would range from sitting *shivah* at home to having their name called out in synagogue before the memorial prayer, the *kaddish*. Similarly, a non-Jewish person who lost a Jewish relative would be welcome to join in all such rituals if they wanted to do so. One does not have to be Jewish to be treated with respect and sensitivity.

9

Coming Out,
But Pushed Out?

Locating LGBT+ Jews within the community

The conversation

Let's start with a conversation. Several years ago, at an interfaith seminar, a Reform rabbi was asked: 'How long have there been gay Jews in your congregation?' Without hesitation, the rabbi responded:

> We have had gay Jews as long as we have had Jewish congregations. However, I think that what you are really asking me is: 'When did we start accepting LGBT – Lesbian, Gay, Bisexual and Transgender – Jews as members of our congregations?' And even then, I would refine your question to say: 'When did we *openly* start accepting LGBT Jews as members of our congregations?'

The Reform rabbi was making a point: that whether closeted or deliberately overlooked, until the latter half of the twentieth century, LGBT+ individuals were present within the Jewish community, even if no one wanted to admit it. Whether it was the rabbi or communal leader who was 'too busy to start a family', the son of a leading member of the synagogue who was 'a confirmed bachelor', the older women who 'lived together as spinsters' having 'missed their window for marriage', all were accepted without too many questions being asked. But as society started to change, so did people's awareness and their discussions.

The approach of Progressive Judaism – of striving to balance tradition with modernity – has always enabled a conversation. At times, this conversation has been a passionate debate as rabbis and congregants have grappled with a society in a state of flux. At others, this conversation has been a dialogue about how Judaism continues to evolve in order to meet the challenges of a changing world. Arguably, over the past forty years, the very best demonstration of this conversation has been the way gay, lesbian and transgender Jews have been included in synagogue life. Which is why all of these contemporary conversations must be located within the eroding conservative discourse of not only a homophobic secular society, but a heteronormative Judaism.

In the closet

To have a conversation with a rabbi that involves the words 'gay' alongside the phrase 'included in synagogue life' is something that many did not believe would be possible in their lifetime. Gerrard, in his seventies, explains:

> When I was in my twenties, I knew that I was gay. To keep up the pretence I dated Jewish girls, but I never married. The truth is that I had a terrifying secret, one that I

couldn't share with my closest relatives, let alone my rabbi. I would not just have been shunned and hated, I may have been incarcerated as a criminal, or institutionalised as mentally defective. I didn't need anyone else to hate me, for I despised myself – for what I was and what I did.

In the Jewish community, there has long been a bigoted intolerance, even hatred of gay people. This stems back to biblical days when sexual intercourse between males was not about love, but about power. In Genesis 19:1–11, the men of Sodom attempt to rape some male visitors who have strayed into their city. This male rape is a conscious form of patriarchal domination. The even earlier biblical narrative, when Ham sees his drunken father Noah and mocks him in front of his brothers, is likewise about power, nudity, male sexual vulnerability and the violation of taboos. Modern academics are clear that the reader is only given half the story about what occurs between Ham and Noah – most likely because the details are too offensive to share. Certainly, in other ancient texts from the same part of the world, male rape and the castration of fathers by their sons is a common theme, for example Uranus and Chronos in Greek mythology. Perhaps this is the reason why there are so few recorded episodes of overt male intercourse in the Bible. What is more, there appear to have been male cult prostitutes, who were condemned in the Bible for their idolatrous ways (Deuteronomy 23:18). Whilst we may never have a clear understanding of the thinking behind the biblical prohibitions against male–male sexual intercourse, the list of commandments that focus on sexual propriety, repeated twice in Leviticus (chapters 18 and 20) appear to prohibit male to male sexual intercourse, condemning the act as *to'evah* – 'an abomination' (Leviticus 18:22 and 20:13).

It is this word, more than any other, which has hounded LGBT+ Jews and non-Jews throughout the centuries. As recently as 1971, the then Chief Rabbi, Dr Immanuel Jakobovits, wrote this in his entry on Homosexuality in the *Encyclopaedia Judaica*:

> Jewish law…rejects the view that homosexuality is to be regarded merely as a disease or as morally neutral… Jewish law holds that no hedonistic ethic, even if called 'love', can justify the morality of homosexuality any more than it can legitimise adultery or incest or polygamy.[1]

Were a British Chief Rabbi to publish something this close-minded in contemporary times, he would be openly condemned for his homophobia. How far we have come in just a few decades, as Charlie reminds us:

> We had to live a clandestine life. If we were outed at work, or at home, or at school, or at synagogue, we would have lost everything. The hatred was everywhere; the police, the government, the church, the rabbinate and the press. You didn't just hear the words 'God hates gays', you believed them.

What about love?

Just as there have always been examples of overt or implicit same-sex love in the secular world, there have always been examples of same-sex affection in Judaism. From the

---

1   Jakobovits, I., 'Homosexuality', in *Encyclopaedia Judaica*, 2nd edn, Vol. 8 (1971, Jerusalem: Keter Publishing House), pp.961–962.

Bible stories of David and his close friend Jonathan, to the talmudic tales of Rabbi Yochanan and his companion Resh Lakish, and from there to the medieval love poems of Rabbis Ibn Gabriol, Shmuel HaNagid, Yehuda HaLevi and Ibn Ezra, men have declared their love for other men. Whether this affection has extended as far as some would suggest, to same-sex attraction, intimacy and partnership, is a matter for academic debate. What is clear is that alongside the apparent biblical prohibitions against male–male intercourse and the talmudic extension to include acts of lesbianism, there have always been known examples of same-sex relationships, many venturing beyond the platonic.

Like Lord Alfred Douglas's notorious phrase 'the love that dare not speak its name',[2] these examples have been silenced so that they have been excluded from the conversation. Within the Orthodox world, there was a strong denial that homosexuality existed, for it was too terrible a sin to imagine.

In contrast, in Reform Judaism, the conversation around how to deal with same-sex love has grown from a silence to a flowing dialogue. There are no known Progressive rabbinic responses to the 1861 removal of the death penalty for homosexuality in the UK, but by the time of the Wolfenden Report in 1957, which argued for the decriminalisation of homosexuality, Progressive rabbis were grappling with these issues.

Unsurprisingly, many of these 1950s and 1960s conversations would appear to the modern reader to be steeped in homophobia, and yet, these heterosexual cis-gender

---

2   Douglas, A., 'Two Loves', in *The Chameleon*, December 1984 edition.

male rabbis (i.e. those who were assigned male at birth and have maintained the same gender identity) were on the whole trying to balance tradition, modernity and compassion. Certainly, by the late 1960s with the ensuing sexual revolution, there were different voices entering the conversation, albeit that they were often met with a harsh backlash by the proponents of late-Victorian morality, claiming to echo the teachings of the Bible. Most Reform rabbis of the 1970s, if pushed, would have been able to identify homosexual individuals and couples within their congregations, but many sustained a conscious blind spot.

Out of the blue

The first openly gay rabbi in the UK was Rabbi Lionel Blue (ordained in 1960). Lionel could never claim to be the first gay rabbi, rather, as he was quick to point out, he was the first one to be open about his sexuality. For Lionel, even his coming out, although an open secret amongst the Reform leadership and his BBC broadcasting bosses, was a case of speaking before he was outed in 1988:

> It was a forbidden subject, you didn't dare. You have to remember, it was a criminal offence in England unless you lived in a certain type of society – café society – where things like Noel Coward existed. But if you lived in middle-class suburbia, it was impossible.[3]

From that moment on, Lionel became the voice of the Jewish lesbian and gay community in the UK. Had Lionel

---

3   Blue, L., *Rainbow Jews: Celebrating LGBT Jewish History and Heritage in the UK* (2014, London: Rainbow Jews), p.5.

been a gay rabbi and not a rabbi who happened to be gay, then his career may well have been over. But Lionel was a respected voice in the national media, as well as a gentle and compassionate interfaith relationship builder; so, his voice was a hard one to exclude from the public and Jewish discourse.

Whilst Lionel, through publications like *Godly and Gay*[4] was a participant in the official conversation inside the room, those on the outside, especially Jewish lesbian feminists, were raising their voices. As Josie puts it:

> We started organising, ensuring that our congregations could no longer ignore us or pretend that we didn't exist. Like the ordination of women rabbis, we were a social injustice that needed to be challenged and, rather than being silenced, we became increasingly vocal. The printed word became our voice, as well as the public arena in which we could and would protest.

Josie and her fellow activists had an uphill struggle. They were discriminated against by the law through various sexual prohibitions, which were not decriminalised until 1967 and, even then, not fully redressed until the age of consent was equalised in 2001. At the same time, they lacked employment rights, which were only introduced in 1999 and extended under the UK's Equality Act of 2010. It took until the twenty-first century for same-sex marriage to be introduced, alongside other progressive advances such as not being penalised for being 'out' in the military,

---

4   Blue, L., *Godly and Gay* (1981, London: Gay Christian Movement).

or a school teacher not risking their job by supporting a struggling LGBT+ student.

For LGBT+ Jews, not only were their relationships either condemned or ignored, alongside their lacking rights and legal protection, but all around them the Jewish world screamed at them to be silent and invisible, or to burn like the proverbial Sodomites. As Gordon recalls:

> We were either invisible or were thrown out. Society was against gay rights, and that included the Jewish community who were just as condemning, couching their prejudice in so-called 'family values'. I will never be able to forget the homophobic rants I heard in the synagogue, or from my father at our *Shabbat* table, or in my home from various friends of my parents. They hated us – but they didn't realise that 'us' included 'me'. They just wanted us to go away and shut up.

However, LGBT+ Jews were not going to go quietly. They wanted a conversation. Since 1972, the Jewish Gay Group (now known as the Jewish LGBT+ Group) has existed. Initially, what has become the world's oldest Jewish association for LGBT+ Jews was established as a secret group, meeting in a small apartment in Clapham. By the early 1980s the group had found its public voice and was openly meeting in a Reform synagogue in Golders Green as well as in Soho. As Rabbi Mark Solomon, the first Orthodox rabbi to come out, recalls, 'The very first meeting I ever came to was the men's pub evening at the King's Arms. I met someone and fell in love. That was pretty dramatic.'[5]

---

5   Solomon, M., in *Rainbow Jews Exhibition: Themed Panels* (2013, London: Rainbow Jews), p.5.

The key conversation of the 1980s was about the ordination of lesbian and gay rabbis. In 1984 Sheila Shulman and Elli Tikvah Sarah, without having discussed it, both applied to Leo Baeck College to commence the five-year programme to become rabbis. Neither had an easy ride as both were kept on probation throughout the full five-year journey. They were left uncertain, until the very last minute, about whether they would be ordained in 1989 and, even then, only after a heated debate amongst their (almost entirely male) future colleagues. It cannot be overstated how their pioneering journey has transformed the modern Progressive rabbinate. Since their brave struggle, well over twenty openly lesbian women and gay men, as well as those self-identifying as bisexual, have been ordained in the UK.

Training LGBT+ rabbis and employing them are very different conversations. There is no doubt that, more often than not, the UK's Liberal Movement led the way, offering employment and acceptance almost a decade faster than its Reform counterpart. In the late 1990s, there were some public cases of employment discrimination that would be challenged today on serious legal grounds under the Equality Act. As Rabbi Indigo Jonah Raphael (who at the time was pre-transition and known then as Rabbi Melinda Carr[6]) explained to us:

> In January 2000 I applied for the post of Principal Rabbi and in April the post was offered to me, subject to the approval of members at a General Meeting.

---

6   This title is in Rabbi Indigo Jonah Raphael's own phrasing, as disclosing a person's pre-transition name/s without their consent is disrespectful and can be illegal.

Unfortunately, things did not run smoothly, culminating in my not being appointed to the post. A quarter-page apology appeared in the *Jewish Chronicle*: apologising for the mismanagement of the appointments process, for: 'unwarranted intrusion into aspects of [my] private life during the interview process' and expressing regret that some members: 'were permitted to express, in a very public fashion, intolerant and discriminatory sentiments'. I was also given a private Letter of Recommendation to give prospective employers. It mentioned that although I'd met all the criteria required for the post of Principal Rabbi... and was unanimously recommended for the position by the Interview Panel and the Council overwhelmingly supported this recommendation, the appointments process had been mismanaged and although 63.3% of the members voted in favour of my appointment, 'no effect was given to the appointment'. It stated that the failure to appoint was: 'in no way connected to [my] abilities...' and acknowledged that this 'led to wide spread publicity both locally, nationally and internationally'. Every time my name and title were mentioned in the press they were now being prefaced by my sexuality, like this part of my life had become compulsory public fodder. I have never shown anyone the letter. The whole situation was an incredibly painful and life changing process. I take some comfort that, out of this process, certain lessons were learned.

Back then it was acceptable to seek a 'family man' to fill a rabbinic post. The implicit message was that the congregation would not hire a gay man or a woman, let alone a lesbian – only a straight, male rabbi would suffice.

Many LGBT+ rabbis still bear the scars of their very public, or covered-up, experiences of having been passed over for a congregational job at which they would have excelled.

Even now, nearly thirty years since the ordination of Rabbis Sheila Shulman and Elli Tikvah Sarah, not every Progressive synagogue would readily employ an openly LGBT+ rabbi. And yet, this too is only a matter of time as more and more LGBT+ rabbis are ordained. Many congregations have come a very long way in just a few decades; some have gone from having a homophobic blow-out to now employing a much-loved LGBT+ rabbi. Through this process of evolution, rather than revolution, one by one, the so-called 'pink-glass ceilings' are being shattered. What is more, very few denominations of any religion have made as much progress in as short a time. As one male rabbi recently remarked:

> No one seems to care that I have a boyfriend rather than a girlfriend. What people want to know is whether I'm good at my job and whether I care about repairing a broken world. Some members even tell me that my 'life experience' is an advantage, making me a better, more compassionate rabbi.

Another rabbi was less positive, explaining that:

> As a woman and as a lesbian I always have so much to prove. Many congregants are very positive, but for some, they get so distracted by my gender or sexuality or even what I wear, that they lose sight of my skills and experience.

AIDS

The ordination of lesbian and gay rabbis did not occur in a vacuum. The other key conversation of the 1980s and early 1990s was AIDS. The disease was met with hatred rather than compassion. Initially misunderstood as a 'gay flu' or a 'plague from God', the effects were felt everywhere, including within the Jewish community. Suddenly, families who did not know that their sons were gay had to prepare for their imminent death. It was a double shock of the worst kind. The sense of loss was accompanied by shame and guilt, as well as great fear. Joseph recalls:

> People hated us. They assumed that we were all promiscuous and that this was a punishment for our lack of morals. It was wicked and cruel. Everything happened so fast and no one took the time to understand. The media fanned the flames of hatred. People were ashamed to say that we were ill. If you had a mark on your skin everyone assumed that you were going to die. People wouldn't touch each other for fear of catching the modern plague. Those who weren't ill in the gay community cared for the dying, and, afterwards, we were riddled with survivor's guilt. It was the worst time of my life and I lost so many people I loved.

The response from many Progressive synagogues was overwhelmingly positive – pastoral care came before stigma. Reform and Liberal rabbis were sought for their non-judgemental sensitivity, as Patrick said:

> We knew that they would be there for us and see us as people, not as sinners. When our lovers died, they would

bury them without making us invisible. Sometimes they wept with us.

This was a stark contrast to the treatment of many other same-sex mourners who lost their partners. Due to the stigma, they were often ignored by the families of their dead lovers. Forbidden from attending funerals, they were deemed not to be next of kin, which is why some suddenly found themselves thrown out of their shared homes, or sidelined from their partner's families. This double loss was too much to bear – which is why some Progressive rabbis found their pastoral work rapidly increasing as they reached out to support them. In the late 1980s, Rabbi Lionel Blue, together with Reverend Martin Johnson and others, established the first retreat for gay men with HIV-AIDS. As Rabbi Mark Solomon recalls:

> At the time it was a pretty unique thing. There was not much else happening around that time of a religious nature for people with AIDS. It took place somewhere in Somerset once a year, and that was a very powerful experience.[7]

This human face of the rabbinate enabled a welcoming home for gay and lesbian Jews. At last, they could start turning to progressive synagogues, in addition to the UK's dedicated Lesbian and Gay Jewish Helpline.

Returning to the 1990s, with ordination ceasing to be a question and with the slow but steady presence of lesbian and gay rabbis in more and more 'mainstream'

---

7 Solomon, M., in *Rainbow Jews Exhibition: Themed Panels* (2013, London: Rainbow Jews), p.6.

synagogues, focus turned to other national and communal conversations of equality.

Legalised love

As Britain began to debate the rights and wrongs of an equalised age of consent and whether to officially recognise same-sex relationships, so too in the Jewish world were conversations taking place. The rise of Jewish gay and lesbian groups as well as same-sex synagogues and friendship groups, such as Beit Klal Yisrael in Kensington (founded in 1990 by Rabbi Sheila Shulman), created a space for some serious discussions around equality. The hottest topic was finding a Jewish way to celebrate same-sex relationship ceremonies. Within the UK's Reform Movement, officiating at a same-sex ceremony was a guaranteed way for a rabbi to get fired. That didn't stop some rabbis from officiating in private. As early as 1990 Rabbi Sheila Shulman conducted a same-sex commitment ceremony in a private home. Yet, it was time to go public.

Once again, the Liberal Movement led the conversation, with the Reform Movement lagging behind. In 1995 the conversation began in earnest, championed by Rabbi Elli Tikvah Sarah, who was to face a career-changing backlash for pioneering this issue. In 1996, whilst serving as Director of Programmes for the Reform Movement, Elli gave a sermon on *Kol Nidrei* (the holiest night of the Jewish year) at a Reform congregation.[8] Interviewed in 2013 for the Rainbow Jews Project, Rabbi Elli said:

---

8   Sarah, E.T., 'Covenant of Love' in *Trouble-Making Judaism* (2012, London: David Paul Books).

I made a big mistake – to give a sermon on the theme of 'covenant of love'. The minute I mentioned that I was going to give this covenant of love, someone from the congregation stood up and said: 'it is an abomination'... It showed me that this was a big issue. All hell broke loose... I had to give public apologies; it was very humiliating... I tried soldiering on, but I realised that, actually, they'd all be happier if I left.[9]

Rabbi Elli Tikvah Sarah joined Rabbi Mark Solomon in championing the cause of same-sex marriage within the Liberal Movement, but Elli's bravery had started a new conversation within Reform Judaism, one that took on quite a number of nasty tones, before informing a new debate amongst Reform rabbis. In 1998, the working party of the Reform Rabbis' Assembly published a report that intended to help individual Reform rabbis to decide whether to conduct lesbian and gay commitment ceremonies. Yet, according to Rabbi Mark Solomon, gay marriage 'had become a very, very contentious issue and brought out a huge amount of latent homophobia that I don't think anybody realised was still there'.[10]

Despite the heated debates, by the end of the 1990s, Reform rabbis were no longer facing expulsion if they officiated at same-sex ceremonies. This was a significant victory, even though the approved legislation was begrudging and offered more restrictions than permissions. Very few rabbis broke rank to officiate at

---

9   Sarah, E.T., in *Rainbow Jews Exhibition: Summary for Rabbi Elli Tikvah Sarah* (2013, London: Rainbow Jews), p.4.

10 Solomon, M., in *Rainbow Jews – Jewish and Gay: Conflict or Comfort* (2013, London: Rainbow Jews), p.9 of transcript at https://docplayer.net/34263829-Jewish-and-gay-conflict-or-comfort.html

these ceremonies, in part because very few same-sex couples found the restrictive legislation to mirror the ceremony they desired, so they sought officiants from outside the Progressive rabbinate. Once again, Liberal Judaism led the charge, beginning work in 2000 on a same-sex wedding liturgy, which was published in 2005 in anticipation of new government legislation. Radically, this liturgy included the Hebrew word for marriage in its title.

In the same year of 2005, just a few months before the delayed same-sex civil partnership national legislation came into effect, the first same-sex blessing ceremony took place within a Reform synagogue. Ian, one half of the happy couple recalls:

> We were so restricted by what we could and couldn't do. No wedding canopy, no rings, no traditional rituals – now it all seems so unwelcoming, but back then it was radical and controversial. Our three brave women rabbis worked with us to stretch every boundary so that we could have the ceremony of our dreams. Even then, we were under constant threat of having the event ruined if it leaked into the Jewish press. In the end, we held our breath and enjoyed a life-affirming day in our synagogue, surrounded by our loved ones and congregation.

Within two years a same-sex ceremony had taken place in another Reform synagogue that had unknowingly parted with many of the restrictions. As Jim and Martin reflected:

> We didn't realise that we were breaking some of the rules. We had a supportive young rabbi, a community who wanted to celebrate with us and we couldn't have

had a more loving or wonderful day standing under our
huppah [canopy] in our sanctuary. We're so gratified that
our *b'rit ahavah* [covenant of love] helped encourage the
rabbis to effect change for the next generation. When
we devised the ceremony that was exactly our plan, to
lay foundations for the future in the spirit of *tikkun olam*
[repairing a fragmented world].

It is worth noting that even the terms *b'rit ahavah* (covenant of love) and *b'rit ahuvim* (lovers' covenant) were
controversial. In her ground-breaking book, *Engendering
Judaism*, Rachel Adler advocates the use of a *b'rit ahavah*
as a feminist alternative to the transactional contract of
Orthodox marriage.[11] The Reform rabbinic legislation
of the 1990s had been emphatic that the language of
marriage was not allowed to be associated with same-
sex ceremonies. Words such as *kiddushin* (holiness),
the technical name for a religious marriage, were strictly
prohibited. Liberal Judaism's suggestion of using *b'rit
ahavah* was a creative alternative,[12] not least because it
circumvented the issue of there not being a *ketubbah*
(Jewish marriage contract). However, for some, even
a lover's covenant was a step too far, as the term *b'rit*
(covenant) was deemed to be an appropriation of the
sacred bond of marriage, which was solely between a man
and a woman.

---

11 Adler, R., *Engendering Judaism* (1998, Philadelphia, PA: Jewish
    Publication Society).
12 Liberal Judaism, *B'rit Ahavah. Covenant of Love. Seder Kiddushin.
    Service of Commitment for Same-Sex Couples* (2005, London:
    Liberal Judaism).

Nevertheless, this well-publicised ceremony, alongside changing attitudes amongst Reform rabbis, together with serious liturgical advances by mainly Liberal rabbis, led to a new conversation. The Reform rabbis now counted amongst their ranks many recently ordained LGB colleagues. In 2009, a new debate started in earnest. Unlike the tone of the discussions of almost a decade before, things had changed radically. Reform Judaism was now playing catch-up with civil society and the popular civil partnership ceremonies. The discussions of 2009 resulted in a Reform rabbinic resolution that was positive and welcoming and looked forward to a day when full marriage equality could be extended to same-sex couples in UK synagogues. That parity was not to follow until 2014 when the law changed in the UK. Since then dozens of same-sex ceremonies have taken place inside and out of synagogues, as Rebecca and Fiona said:

> How lucky we are to live in such a time of change when we can marry the person we love, standing under a *huppah* with all the traditions of a Jewish ceremony, including exchanging rings and signing a same-sex *ketubbah*.

Same sex, different faiths

Since 2009, further strides have been taken in recognition that only one in ten LGBT+ Jews is likely to find a Jewish partner. As has been examined in detail in Chapter 8, finding a Jewish partner is hard enough if one is heterosexual. To find a same-sex Jewish partner is very rare. This can present all sorts of challenges for LGBT+

Jews, who have had to overcome serious prejudice to feel accepted. Having a non-Jewish partner can be an added pressure and source of pain when facing disapproval from the wider Jewish community, who champion Jewish–Jewish relationships. Accordingly, since 2012, when Reform rabbis started officiating at mixed-faith blessings, there have been ceremonies to celebrate the love of a same-sex Jew and non-Jew. Nicola, one of the first brides to enjoy this new ceremony said:

> 2014 was a momentous year for us as a couple, it was everything I thought we would never have, and so much more than I ever could have imagined. In 2014, I married my German, Catholic but amazingly Jew-'ish' now wife, blessed by a gay rabbi. Since then, we mark all the major festivals and light our weekly *Shabbat* candles. Ironically, I am now more observant than before, and this is driven by my wife!

Visibility

As the national anti-discrimination legislation of the late 1990s and early 2000s took effect, all across British society LGBT+ visibility and acceptance became normative, culminating in the aforementioned 2014 introduction of legal same-sex marriage. In this arena, Progressive synagogues have been the barometer of society, usually a few years ahead, occasionally a couple of years behind but always striving to welcome, where once it shunned. Yet even then, the battle is far from over. As a leading LGBT+ Jewish activist, Peggy Sherwood MBE explains:

The heads of Reform and Liberal Judaism came to the Jewish Gay and Lesbian Group's 40th anniversary in 2012 and I thought: 'How far has the Jewish LGBT world come?' But the day when the [Orthodox] Chief Rabbi comes to a JGLG event, then we'll know we've really arrived.[13]

One of the most significant changes of this decade has been the foundation, in 2011, of KeshetUK, an educational and advocacy charity promoting equality and diversity for lesbian, gay, bisexual and transgender (LGBT+) people in the Jewish and wider communities. KeshetUK's introduction was championed by many Progressive rabbis, who have celebrated the great strides it has made to train congregations and schools in LGBT+ best practice.

One area that is now a given is same-sex families and being sensitive to the needs of the children involved. In many synagogue-based supplementary Religion Schools one can find pupils with two fathers or two mothers, as Kim said:

> My children are just like everyone else's. It took the teacher more time to adjust than the other children or parents. Our rabbi made sure that we were treated just like everyone else, and that's how our children feel. On a good day, they skip into the *Heder* [Sunday school] like all the other children; and on a bad morning, they fight us. In that, as with all aspects of synagogue life, including receiving honours at family services and during festivals,

---

13 Sherwood, P., in *Rainbow Jews Exhibition: Themed Panels* (2013, London: Rainbow Jews), p.8.

we are no different to anyone else. That's what we wanted in a community and we found it.

The Reform *Beit Din* recognises same-sex families in all matters, including surrogacy, adoption and conversion. The numerous Reform converts who identify as LGBT+ are a testament to how far Reform Judaism has come. Judaism does not proselytise, so the fact that so many LGBT+ individuals and couples are making a bee-line for progressive synagogues should speak for itself. Mark had heard positive things about Reform Judaism but had not expected to find such an inclusive environment:

Where I may have had the preconceived idea that religious communities are often not welcoming of LGBT+ people, hearing that not only did this synagogue have female as well as male rabbis (and was therefore egalitarian), but that one of the rabbis was also a gay man, this immediately put my mind at rest and indeed I left those preconceptions at the door.

To provide for their LGBT+ congregants, some Progressive synagogues now hold services to mark Pride, World AIDS Day and other LGBT+ significant occasions, such as recognising homosexual victims of the Nazis on International Holocaust Memorial Day or marking Transgender Day of Remembrance. For many self-identifying cis-gender gay and lesbian Jews, the struggle, at least in the mainstream synagogues, is well on the way to being won. That does not mean that there are not still some challenges, not least tackling LGBT+ poor mental health and finding ways to champion the rights of ageing same-sex couples in an era when there are no LGBT+ welcoming Jewish care homes. And yet, with all these great strides of progress across the decades, there now comes a much-needed change in the tone of the conversation.

Transitioning

The newest frontier for synagogues to traverse is transgender rights. Historically, although categories of gender diversity are mentioned in Jewish literature, there have been two aspects of Jewish law that have led to discrimination against transgender people. In Deuteronomy 22:5, cross-dressing is prohibited, and in the Talmud the prioritisation of male genitalia in discussion about identity leads to a lack of recognition for gender dysphoria. However, as equality legislation has rolled out to include trans individuals, including the UK's Gender Recognition Act in 2004 and Equality Act in 2010, the conversation is evolving into a multi-voiced discussion, requiring further nuance and sensitivity; something often lacking in sensationalist and transphobic media headlines.

In a religious movement that has broken with traditional gender roles (see Chapter 7) and made huge advances in praying without gender-specific liturgy or gender-segregated spaces, it might seem obvious that transphobia would not be acceptable. Unsurprisingly, there have been trans individuals in Reform synagogues for some decades, but only now, as a nuanced understanding of gender identities (binary and non-binary) becomes part of the public discourse, are things starting to develop.

These emerging areas of awareness are slowly changing the Reform landscape. Whether it is making some, or all, of the synagogue's toilets 'gender neutral', rethinking how to use gender pronouns, offering a *B-mitzvah*, alongside a *bar/bat mitzvah* (for thirteen-year-old boys/girls), marking Transgender Day of Visibility or simply offering a safe space, the work is only just beginning. From individual synagogues to Reform Movement-wide infrastructure, there is a great deal to reappraise, not least the traditionally gendered use of Hebrew language which can fail to accommodate a convert whose gender is non-binary and who requires a fitting Hebrew name that includes, rather than excludes them.

As Jon writes:

> When I tell people that I feel accepted and welcomed as a trans person within my Jewish community, they're often surprised. Acceptance of trans people in religious spaces – really? Often, people have the vision of religious institutions as stagnant places filled with old white men pulling the strings and preaching hatred while their congregation nod along. That couldn't be further from the truth I found within Judaism.

Jon's story is an inspiring one, and it is only the beginning of a new chapter that will, within a decade, lead to the ordination of trans rabbis; a decade-old norm in American Reform Judaism. At present, one rabbi, Indigo Jonah Raphael transitioned some years after ordination. Indigo's journey included some very painful experiences in the rabbinate:

> I was asked: 'How can you be transgender and still Jewish?'. I was surprised, disappointed and my sadness was palpable.

It felt like two integral parts of my identity ought to be mutually exclusive: [that] I should choose between the L-G-B-T-Q-I-A-Q and the Jewish community, because it's anathema to be a trans Jew. Missing was recognition that people of faith who are LGBT+ can connect with and feel integrated with both communities... [For] we cannot live our lives for other people, we cannot sacrifice who we are for their sake, to protect them from potential confusion, shame or pain. Nor can we live other people's lives. We can only live our lives and seek to fulfil our unique potential – for only then can we make a congruent contribution.

Whether it's a bespoke naming ceremony, as a poignant marker for someone who has transitioned, or designing a new marriage contract, this new awareness of trans rights brings with it great potential for designing creative rituals and liturgy. Of course, because it is not '*straight*forward' things may not always be simple, for example marriage issues can be confounding, as Ruthie, married to Rabbi Indigo (a trans man) explains:

We have been on a remarkable journey documenting a herstory, history and our story! Because there isn't a single marriage bill, inclusive of same-sex marriage we were faced with a quandary after Indigo transitioned and affirmed his gender identity as male. Having sought legal advice the choices were: either to dissolve our civil partnership and then enter into a marriage (between people of opposite sex) or to keep our civil partnership, enter into a same-sex marriage and then, with Indigo's Gender Recognition Certificate, to convert that into a marriage between people of the opposite sex. We didn't want to break or dissolve our spiritual and legal bond, we didn't see why we should have to.

In the end, I walked into the registry office with my bearded and moustached Beloved and we signed the paperwork to enter into a same-sex marriage! It was a real challenge for our integrity that the law couldn't deal with our situation more appropriately. The nuances of our lives don't fit neatly. At our Renewal of Vows at which a rabbi (who is a friend) officiated, celebrating thirty years together, we reflected proudly that we'll always be a Queer couple!

The conversation continues

Like Rabbis Lionel Blue, Sheila Shulman, Elli Tikvah Sarah and Mark Solomon, Rabbi Indigo's pioneering work is paving the way for the many, many who will follow.

All of these sweeping changes have come about through the courage of individuals and the steady beat of civil progress. At times, there have been long, protracted and painful debates, mirroring the public discourse; at other times there have been discussions during which there has been an obvious meeting of progressive hearts and minds. The result is a Reform Movement that no longer just tolerates or patronisingly welcomes LGBT+ individuals. Such is the nature of the affirmative and celebratory embrace of the LGBT+ community that when entering a synagogue in an urban area and attending a baby blessing, *bar/bat/B-mitzvah* or a ceremony of welcome for a new convert, it comes as little or no surprise that either the individual, their parents or, indeed, their rabbi do not conform to the heteronormative stereotypes of Reform congregations a mere forty-odd years ago.

It has been a long conversation; often radical, always governed by Jewish values and far from over whilst prejudice and phobia still exist, but, ultimately, paving the way for a brave new world.[14]

---

14 We are most grateful to Rabbi Elli Tikvah Sarah, Rabbi Mark Solomon, Rabbi Indigo Jonah Raphael and Zachary Carruthers for their invaluable advice as we wrote this chapter.

10

Changing Others to Brothers (and Sisters)

Welcoming those who do not fit the stereotype

The other

The Hebrew word for 'other' is *acher*. Otherness, aside from the various philosophical and political definitions, is about being perceived to be different from the norm. In synagogues throughout the world, being 'other' can be a daunting experience, not least where conformity is expected in terms of family make-up, religious practice and ethnic background. Throughout this book we have addressed areas of potential otherness. In some cases, the experiences of 'other' groups warrants a dedicated chapter, for example LGBT+ Jews (Chapter 9). In this section we explore the experiences of a variety of 'others' who can expect a warmth of welcome that may be tepid, at best, in many areas of the Jewish world.

Single parents

They say that it takes a village or community to raise a child. Parenting when you are on your own can be a wonderful, challenging, rewarding experience. Sometimes, single parents are dealing with a divorce; sometimes, they are left picking up the pieces when a spouse dies or leaves the country; sometimes, there are individuals who make the decision to go it alone and have a child with the aid of modern medicine; and sometimes, there are people who find themselves unexpectedly pregnant and all alone.

For each of these single parents a Jewish community can feel very hostile, geared towards happy families, suspicious of those who are deemed to have failed to match that image. Sometimes this is overtly expressed, whilst at other times the person concerned can sense it. Irrespective, this is highly unpleasant and hurtful at the very time when someone needs to feel supported. All this can result in single parents dropping out of communal life, mainly because they feel that they are not wanted or, perhaps worse, are shameful. In reality, of course, it is the community that should be ashamed. Quite apart from causing distress to struggling individuals, we lose both them and their children. By contrast, what we need to do is offer a wonderful support network.

For Talia, finding a friendly ear was critical:

> My husband had recently walked out, and I was struggling in every way possible, particularly financially. My children were old enough to attend a Religion School, but I couldn't afford the fees. There were days when I felt so alone, and I didn't want to burden my ageing parents with the depth of my sorrow. I reached out to my Reform rabbi. She was

understanding and promised to find ways to help us. She found a way to waive most of the synagogues fees and also made an extra effort to make my children feel that she was there for them too. She was incredible, and she gently found a way to connect me up with another single mum. Looking back on that time, I thank God for sending her my way.

As you will read throughout this chapter, offering decent pastoral support is not exclusive to Reform Judaism. Yet, it is when there may be a religious challenge alongside a pastoral need, that the Reform approach can make all the difference. Later in this chapter we deal with divorce and being a widow/widower. For now, we want to focus on the issues of teenage pregnancy and those who choose to have children without a co-parent.

Nigel was distraught when Miranda, his seventeen-year-old daughter fell pregnant and was adamant that she was keeping the baby. The father of the baby was not on the scene. Fortunately, Nigel had a good relationship with his rabbi:

I made an appointment and went to see my rabbi. He's always been so supportive and was very good when Miranda had her *bat mitzvah*. We talked through the options and he helped me to make peace with her decision.

Miranda was very relieved and came to see the rabbi:

He didn't make me feel judged for wanting to keep the baby. We discussed the option of an abortion and he

> explained how, in Reform Judaism, the commandment
> to 'choose life' could also be interpreted as choosing my
> quality of life. In the end, I decided to keep the baby, but I
> know that my rabbi would have supported me either way.
> Since Chloe was born, the whole community has made
> her feel so welcome and loads of our friends came to her
> baby blessing.

For Nigel, Miranda and Chloe, it all worked out in the end. At the other end of the spectrum to teenage pregnancy is the challenge for those women who have always wanted a family but have never met the right partner and are aware that their fertile years are finite. Some may opt for the wonderful *mitzvah* (good deed) of adoption – this topic is dealt with at the end of Chapter 5 – whilst others will want to take advantage of the amazing developments in fertility medicine. That is why, more and more women in their thirties and forties are going down the route of artificial insemination via a sperm bank.

Outside of marriage, Orthodox Jewish law rarely advocates the use of IVF and other fertility treatment. In fact, most rabbinic authorities would not condone single-parent artificial insemination. However, Reform Judaism champions personal autonomy and the responsible use of technological developments. Roxie's story is a good example of how this can work well:

> I'd spent nearly twenty years trying to date Jewish men.
> My parents started mentioning my 'biological clock' and
> whilst I would find it infuriating, part of me knew that they
> were right. At thirty-six, I had several of my eggs frozen.

When I turned forty, I got back in touch with the fertility clinic and we sourced a viable, anonymous sperm donor. It was scary to think that I was going to do this alone. My parents were with me at every step, as was the social worker in my synagogue. When Nathan was born, the social worker and rabbi came to the hospital to support us both. The rabbi arranged Nathan's ritual circumcision and now, a few years later, everyone cannot believe that Nathan has just started his first term at Religion School. He is no different to any of the other kids in his class, and the other parents have been incredibly welcoming. My parents have had a few rather insensitive comments from some of their so-called friends, but, overall, everyone has been amazing. An older gay couple at the synagogue have become Nathan's honorary uncles.

A happy ending, but what might have happened if Talia, Miranda or Roxie had faced a closed door? Our tradition teaches us that 'all the family of Israel are responsible for one another' (Talmud Shavuot 39a), that responsibility must not stop when an individual's circumstances do not neatly align with conventional and historical approaches to Jewish family life. Frankly, with the growing numbers of single parents, a far more proactive approach is needed to support them, so that, as a community, we can help to raise the next generation of young Jews.

The unmarried

In many Orthodox synagogues it is traditional for un-married men not to wear a *tallit* (prayer shawl). Likewise, it is expected that only married women will cover their heads with a hat or scarf. For those who have yet to meet their future spouse, or who have chosen not to marry, this can present quite a challenge. No doubt, one of the origins of these customs was to help identify those who were single in order to assist them with finding a partner. Likely, the merits of this simple system were considered before any embarrassment and pain that the 'singling out' of singles might cause. For the LGBT+ Jew, forbidden from marrying a partner of the same sex, this system would be a badge of shame. Likewise, for the bachelor or spinster who never met 'Mr or Miss Right'. Fortunately, in Reform synagogues women are not expected to wear a hat and anyone, irrespective of their gender, can wear a *kippah* (ritual head covering). Likewise, anyone Jewish over the age of *bar/bat mitzvah* (thirteen years old) is welcome to wear a *tallit*. In these simple, yet significant ways, no one is made to feel like an 'other'. Take Roseanne:

> When I was in my twenties, I was madly in love with a man. I thought he was wonderful and so I was over the moon when he proposed. Unfortunately, he turned out to be a love rat – he was married to someone else and had been carrying on with several other people behind my back. I was heartbroken – it took many years to get over it. So, I threw myself into my career and one day, several decades later, I realised that I was of an age when I was unlikely to meet my soul mate. For years I had faced the shame of attending *shul* [synagogue] with my sisters on the festivals and being the only woman my age who wasn't wearing a hat. I felt lots of eyes on me. Someone tried to match-make, but I felt that it was done out of pity,

and when I arrived at the first blind date it was obvious that we never going to be compatible. Three years ago, one of my divorced girlfriends invited me to spend *Rosh Hashanah* [the Jewish New Year] at her synagogue, which was Reform. For the first time in decades I felt anonymous and that no one could peg me as 'that lonely spinster'. It was liberating,

For those like Roseanne, coming to a congregation where they can self-identify without stigma can be a breath of fresh air. Everyone has their story and not all individuals want a partner. At the same time, Jewish matchmaking is a *mitzvah* (good deed). Provided that this is organised in an appropriate way, ensuring that those wishing to be introduced to potential dates have given their express consent, there is nothing wrong with trying to help people find love. Many synagogues offer opportunities for singles to meet one another. When it works, it can be a source of utter joy. As Jonny, one half of a recently married couple said:

When I first came to the synagogue, I was very keen to meet a nice Jewish girl. Heather was introduced to me by the rabbi, and although it took us a few dates to find that deeper connection, we've never looked back. It's hard to believe that was three years ago, and now we've been married for six months. Our wedding took place in the synagogue where we met. The rabbi said such lovely things about how, in Jewish tradition, the successful pairing of souls is as much of a challenge for God as was splitting the Red Sea during the Exodus.

The divorced

Just a few decades ago, divorce was almost socially unacceptable. Divorcing couples were seen as irresponsible and, where there were children involved, the parents were accused of not putting the children first. In fact, the contrary may be true and we often hear that remaining in an unhappy marriage has been destructive for all those caught in the crossfire.

In Reform Judaism we recognise that divorce is not only permitted but can be the right course to pursue in various circumstances. We would term divorce as a 'sad but necessary deed' when a marriage has broken down and is beyond repair. Chaining together people who are unhappily married is a disaster for all concerned. In Chapter 2 we addressed the issue of *agunah* – the chained wives of Orthodox Jewish men who have been refused a divorce by their bitter and recalcitrant spouses. Reform Judaism has found a way around this issue. Likewise, Reform Judaism has found a compassionate way to enable a divorcee to marry a *cohen* (a descendant of a priest – see Chapter 2). For some, this prohibition has caused so much pain – forcing them to choose between the person they love and the synagogue they call their spiritual home. Take Graham for example:

> When I was a child, my father and grandfather showed me how to lead the special prayer of the *cohanim* [the priests]. I was proud to be a *cohen* and to take a leading role in my synagogue. That all changed in my thirties when I fell in love with Denise. She comes from a nice Jewish family and has three wonderful children. Unfortunately, her first marriage was an unhappy one and fell apart just after the

birth of her younger son. We met about a year later. I was a bit of a late starter and Denise was the first person I'd ever felt that way about. We wanted to get married, but I was told that I'd have to forfeit my role as a *cohen* and that any future children would carry a stigma. Everyone was deeply unhappy, and Denise and I even spent a few weeks apart. But then we realised we couldn't live without each other.

In the end, it was Graham's father who picked up the phone to a Reform rabbi. The rest was straightforward. Two years later Graham and Denise were married at the Reform synagogue. Fifteen years later, their son became *bar mitzvah* in front of the same congregation. As Denise commented:

It all worked out in the end. We belong to a lovely Reform synagogue. Graham's parents have remained members of their Orthodox synagogue, but at his grandson's Reform *bar mitzvah*, Graham's father was the proudest person in the room.

Reform Judaism, with its pragmatic, people-first approach, works well for those who have an unsolvable halakhic problem. Yet religious reasons are not the only grounds for a divorced man or woman to find a congregation that will accept them. Despite the high divorce rate, including within the Jewish community, for some, divorce still carries a stigma. Cheryl felt uncomfortable:

The first Sabbath after we'd announced that we were divorcing, I went to synagogue. It was obvious that several people were talking about me, but I decided to tough it out. When, many weeks later, the gossip still hadn't died down, I'd had enough. I didn't want to be somewhere where I, or my children, would be judged.

Due to the way that Reform Judaism has always striven to balance tradition with modernity, balancing science and faith, ritual and reason, the kind of people who are attracted to Reform congregations tend to be on the more liberal end of the spectrum, ideologically, if not always politically. For this reason, Reform congregations are a reflection of the society in which they exist. At any time, in any service, one can find divorced families. There are plenty of divorced people in Orthodox congregations and plenty of divorced Orthodox and Reform rabbis. Yet it can often take a less conformist community to offer people like Cheryl the inclusive spiritual haven which they seek.

The bereaved

In any congregation, at any moment, there will be people with broken hearts as the result of the death of a loved one. Often, Judaism is held up for the thoughtful way it demarcates the year of mourning into clear and helpful stages: the very intense first week, the rest of that month, the next eleven months, the anniversaries. Rather than suppressing grief, Jewish ritual can help the grieving process by offering opportunities to acknowledge one's loss, such as lighting a memorial candle, reciting the mourners' *kaddish* and saying prayers on the anniversary of losing a loved one.

Throughout Scripture, Jewish ethical teachings command us not to oppress the widow or the orphan; more than that, we must support and embrace them during their time of great pain and hardship. The same consideration applies to others who are in a vulnerable state. In all synagogues, mourners are recognised, and their spiritual needs are considered. Often, the same can be said for their pastoral needs, although the quality of care and support may not be universal.

Evading and avoiding the bereaved is nothing new – we have all struggled with finding the right words of condolence in a difficult situation. Of course, there is always some way to be supportive, but this can become an issue for certain people when an individual has suffered an especially complex loss or may be stuck in their grief many years after the death of their loved one. This is where caring communities and rabbis can step up, for each of us grieves in our own way. Take Juliet's story:

> Out of the blue, at fifty-one, Andrew was diagnosed with cancer. Our life changed course dramatically. He died suddenly, traumatically. I was considering converting to Judaism at the time, but my world had fallen apart. I met the rabbi just days after Andrew's death. Fast-forward a few years, and because of the rabbis at my synagogue, I have had support, love and friendship that I would never have imagined. No one at my synagogue knew Andrew, but through the rituals and remembrances I have been able to find a sense of peace.

Alongside appropriate pastoral care, some Reform communities will offer a bereavement support group, or the opportunity to create a bespoke grieving ritual with a rabbi. All of this can help, not least because it will stem from a place of concern and non-judgement.

Occasionally, Jewish law creates a barrier at a time when we most need the support of our community, as Brenda recalls:

> My husband was not Jewish, and he was an atheist. When he died so suddenly of a heart attack, we were in shock. This was compounded when our rabbi refused to attend the funeral, although he rang me to offer his condolences. He also refused to allow us to be buried together. I wanted to arrange prayers in my home, but my children and I were told that this was inappropriate. We felt utterly lost and very let down by the congregation where our two boys had marked their *bar mitzvahs*. A friend told us about a local Reform rabbi who would enable us to be buried side by side. I rang that rabbi and have never looked back. She came straight over and helped us to plan an appropriate funeral, as well as prayers in our home. She was so kind and supportive. It was strange to have never considered joining her congregation. When I did, I never once felt judged by anyone and have made a lifelong friendship with a lady who was also saying *kaddish* for her husband throughout my year of mourning.

Like our grief, our families do not always fit into neat boxes. For people like Brenda and for all sorts of others struggling with the religious and pastoral challenges of bereavement, a Reform synagogue can provide a non-judgemental, person-centred and supportive community.

People of colour

In synagogues of almost every denomination of Judaism you will meet people of colour. In Reform Judaism, we are passionately committed to equality and to seeing each person as having been created in 'God's image', going right back to the very first humans in Genesis.

Clearly, if all of us have features resembling God, irrespective of our height, gender, facial differences and skin colour, then God must have seven billion faces. A simpler view is to see every soul as a reflection of God. Irrespective of whether being created in God's image can be glimpsed on our face or in our heart – *all* of us are equally of God. That is why the traditional discriminatory categories of race and racism have no place in a synagogue. As Lewis explains:

> When I walk into a service and see other people of colour it makes me feel that right here is a place where I can be myself, free from racism. Some of my fellow non-white congregants were born Jewish, other have converted into such a welcoming Jewish tradition. Sometimes we catch each other's eyes and smile, knowing that we all feel the same thing.

Sadly, it has not always been this way. Many synagogues of all denominations have had to counter internal racism and prejudice. What was once acceptable is no longer tolerated. And yet, there are still some corners of the Jewish world where the abhorrent practices of discrimination and derogatory remarks are not altogether eradicated.

Kathy – who has an Afro-Caribbean mother and an Asian father – was interested in converting to Judaism. She went along to a non-progressive service:

> The people at the door seemed friendly. In the middle of the service the rabbi began a really interesting sermon

on the story of Miriam turning white with leprosy, all because she gossiped about the black wife of Moses. But then the rabbi said that the punishment was for Miriam's gossip, not for her views on whether Moses should have married someone who was of a different race. Suddenly, I felt my heart racing. The rabbi went on to make some deeply offensive comments. I don't think he was aware of what he was saying, and the racist nature of his remarks, but that was the last time I went to his synagogue. A few weeks later I went to another synagogue. To my delight, the *bar mitzvah* boy came from a dual-heritage family. Then I noticed that the Warden who was helping him was from an Indian family. At *kiddush* [the refreshments after the service] I got chatting to two other Afro-Caribbean women who had recently converted. I felt like I had come home.

For Kathy, and for the many Jews of colour who are part of our congregations, especially those Jews-by-choice who have added and enriched our congregations through their holy acts of conversion, we strive to build communities where all are equal, valued and welcome.

People with poor mental health

For as long as there have been Jews, there have been Jewish mental health issues. King Saul, Jonah, Elijah and various other biblical characters exhibit classic signs of poor mental health, including anxiety, stress, depression, bipolar disorder and mild schizophrenia. Whilst we know that 'there is nothing new under the sun' (Ecclesiastes 1:9), and that the author of these words encountered the darker days in life, it is only in more recent times that we have begun to regard mental wellbeing as an area requiring serious communal pastoral support. And yet, it is hardly a new issue, not least because breakdowns, depressive episodes, self-harm and suicide have long been visible amongst congregants. Take, for example, the years surrounding the two world wars when many of the returning Jewish soldiers were suffering from post-traumatic stress disorder. The difference is that now, at long last, what was once visible, but unmentionable, is part of an open conversation in every area of the Jewish community, from the school room to the synagogue.

In every community, there will be congregants struggling with their mental wellbeing. Take Charles, who writes:

> I have had a long history of mental health problems. I think, looking back, that I first began to suffer from depression when I was a teenager. I felt like a speck of dust in a hurricane, a drop of water in an ocean, insignificant, and alone. As a young adult, I remember leaving the apartment one Saturday morning and thinking, 'What's the point? Where am I going?' I went back to bed and stayed there for the rest of the weekend. Between 2006 and 2011, I was housebound with depression and anxiety. I only left the house to walk my dog around the block; always at quiet times to avoid contact with other people. After some years I found my way into a Reform synagogue. One of the first things that struck me about the community was its inclusion and diversity. I started going to services regularly and have made quite a few like-minded friends. Where before I have been plagued

with negative patterns of thought and would often find myself trapped in an internal dialogue of self-criticism and talking myself down; I now draw strength from Jewish prayers.

Within British Jewry there are several excellent charities focused on supporting individuals to manage their mental wellbeing. Newer initiatives include Mental Health First Aid courses, which are being run in synagogues to train staff, clergy and volunteers. Likewise, some congregations are running inclusive services or creating safe spaces to enable open, honest and safe conversations. Jo, a leading social worker, employed by a Reform synagogue, explained:

In our changing, more pressurised country, with a cash-strapped NHS and under-resourced social services, despite the best efforts of the public sector, there are too many people falling through the social care net. Mental health is only one of several pastoral areas where the synagogue community must pick up when the statutory services are overstretched. Caring communities are not just inclusive places, they are active and proactive in supporting their most vulnerable and needy members. The growth across the last five years of social care co-ordinators in almost every major Reform synagogue, is not just a nice idea, it's an essential one. Jews are as likely as any other community to suffer poor mental health or be at risk. Prioritising good mental health and wellbeing is for everyone. It's an absolute necessity for an inclusive and caring community to step up; this saves lives.

There is a growing awareness around young people's mental health and the need to support them through the struggles of the teenage years. In Reform summer camps and youth clubs, great care is taken to offer these younger members a space to feel secure and supported. Take the young woman with anorexia who is enabled to participate in a fortnight away from home, or the young man who self-harms. By bringing these issues out into the open, but in an appropriate and non-judgemental manner, more and more of those invisible members with hidden issues are finding that their spiritual home is a caring and supportive one. Sometimes, it can be a lifesaver.

In many countries suicide is a crime, which can lead people to mask their desperation and then it is too late. The traditional Jewish approach to suicide has been to condemn it as a sin. In some Orthodox Jewish cemeteries there is a burial space across a wall or a path that is designated for those who, in their despair, have taken their own lives. This separation symbolises the traditional stigma of suicide and the lack of awareness around mental health. Not only is this separation punitive, but it adds extra distress to mourners at one of the most devastating moments in their lives when they will be struggling with all sorts of unanswerable questions. Their grief will be mixed with confusion and compounded by guilt. Reform Judaism rejects this cruel practice. We recognise that suicide is an act of desperation and that no one in their 'right mind' would take their life, so we treat all cases of suicide as death through mental ill health. As with all other illnesses, we bury with dignity and compassion, both for the sake of the individual concerned and for the family.

Of course, understanding and dedicated pastoral support can be found in many communities across the Jewish spectrum, but the strong focus on pastoral training for Reform rabbis, and the passionate commitment to building caring, inclusive and non-judgemental communities, means that many of those who suffer from mental health-related concerns will make a bee-line for a Reform synagogue.

From other…to brother

Returning to the Hebrew word for 'other' – *acher* – many Hebrew words have shared connections with those from a similar root; sometimes these connections are obvious, in other instances they are more tenuous. The Hebrew word for 'my brother' is *achi.* Whilst *acher* and *achi* are not directly connected, it may be no accident that when the last letter of the Hebrew word *acher* is changed from something impersonal to something directly related – *my* brother – the other is no longer a stranger. In Reform congregations we reach out to the other so that when we find a way to relate, like brothers, we are thereafter connected. To all the 'others' who are reading this – come and join the family – you'll be most welcome.

11

The Curious Attitude to Conversion

Dismantling the 'No entry' signs we have erected

If you approach a Church of England vicar or a Catholic priest and say you wish to become a Christian, you will be welcomed with a warm smile and open arms. A baptism will be arranged, perhaps preceded by a course of induction, but not necessarily; congregants will greet you joyfully on your next appearance in church. If you approach a rabbi and say you want to be Jewish, the reaction will be the exact opposite. It usually starts with a sigh. You may well be turned down, or if the rabbi is more positive, told that it is an arduous task and asked if you have really thought it through. If the rabbi is particularly helpful, you will be told to go away and think about it for six months and then see if you still feel the same way.

Six months later, if you come back and still request to convert, then you may receive a grudging acceptance onto a conversion course, but warned that it may be difficult to complete and many people drop out. Before you start, you may well be told that you have to relocate from your home and live in an area of relatively high Jewish density, such as North London or South Manchester. Only that way will you be able to live Jewish life more fully. There is also the warning that at the end of the course, which can be between one and five years, you will face an examination as to your knowledge, observance and sincerity. It is made clear that although you could pass and become Jewish, you may be failed or told to study for longer. As Reg said after he had been told the above:

> I was shocked. It meant giving up my home, leaving local friends, probably changing my job and possibly finding out in five years' time that it had all been for nothing. If the plan was to put me off, then it certainly worked!

There may be a case for ensuring that those converting are fully familiar with the faith they are seeking to enter, but this goes far beyond any such diligence and is a clear statement of negativity: for centuries Judaism has been putting up the 'No entry' sign.

A history of conversion

It was not always this way. In biblical times, non-Jews either married into a Jewish family or attached themselves to the faith via the ritual of circumcision. Ruth's famous declaration – 'your people shall be my people, and your God shall be my God' (Ruth 1:16) – was deemed a sufficient declaration of intent. It was as much about joining the tribe as signing up to a belief system. The open welcome accelerated so much in Roman times that the

Gospel writer Matthew was driven to complain that the Pharisees 'travelled over sea and land to make one proselyte' (Matthew 23:15). Even if this was hyperbole, Judaism attracted a considerable number of converts, especially as belief in the Greek and Roman gods crumbled during this period.

This trend was reversed by two external factors: first, the war with Rome in 67 CE led to Jews being regarded as a rebellious element within the empire and, therefore, less attractive to those who wished to advance socially or politically; second, the rise of Christianity offered a form of monotheism but without some of the impedimentary rituals, such as the dietary laws or circumcision. This slowdown then ground to a halt when the emperor Constantine converted to Christianity and went on to ban conversion to Judaism. This external intervention was then internalised and transformed into a lack of desire by Jewish authorities to convert others. It was exacerbated by the fact that Jews largely lived outside the Land of Israel, scattered throughout the Roman Empire, guests in strange lands and no longer the majority culture.

The growing social divide – if not outright hostility – during the Middle Ages between Jews and the population in whose midst they lived made the thought of anyone crossing from one community to the other an extreme rarity. Christians were horrified at the thought that one of their number might side with the unbelievers and endanger their mortal soul; Jews were highly suspicious that anyone might wish to join them, as well as fearful of the consequences, be it popular disturbances or action by the authorities. The mutual antipathy towards conversion to Judaism led to the assumption that the readmission of the Jews to England under Cromwell was on condition that they did not 'Judaize'. There is no evidence for this at all, but it was symptomatic of the perception that 'thou shalt not convert others to Judaism'.

Even when applicants for conversion were accepted, it was customary for several decades to send them abroad to Holland to convert there, so that no blame could be attached to British Jewry for taking souls away from the Church.

There was another motive for this reticence: ever since the birth of Christianity and its relentless sense of mission to convert as many others as possible to it, Jews had been the object of evangelisation. This had included compulsory attendance at missionary sermons during the Middle Ages, as well as the choice between converting to Christianity or being expelled from their country of residence. Even when Jews started being accepted by wider society, there were still problems – for the collapse of the ghetto walls not only brought certain freedoms, but also exposed them to less direct but more insidious methods of conversion.

These attempts to proselytise were partly aimed at wealthier Jews, tempting them to gain greater respectability in the social circles to which they aspired. They were also targeted at poorer Jews, whereby soup kitchens gave out missionary tracts with the food they offered, as well as putting on activities to attract Jewish youngsters. The Jewish authorities felt that it would be impossible to protest successfully against such missionary activity, if they themselves were converting Christians. Despite the fact that the Church put considerable manpower and money into their mission to convert the Jews, and although only a few Christians went in the other direction and joined Judaism, and only then without any prompting, there was a strong feeling that if the rabbis were seen to favour conversion to Judaism, then this would undermine their efforts to repel the Christian evangelical agenda.

The gradual acceptance of religious diversity and personal choice within British society meant that this perceived barrier from the non-Jewish side dissipated. However, the objections against conversion from the Jewish community were maintained for another reason: the view that unless a convert was going to be totally observant, it was better that they did not become Jewish and breach the laws. It was deemed preferable that they remained a non-Jew who was not under any obligations, than be Jewish and break some of the commandments. It was thought too difficult to tell in advance whether someone would maintain their observance after conversion, however diligent they might seem during the course, so it was best to reject all but the most exceptional cases. Thus, the default reaction to any enquiries was to turn them down.

This was then justified biblically by the fact that when Naomi's son (Ruth's husband), died and Ruth said she would stay with Naomi rather than return to her own Moabite people, Naomi had tried to dissuade her from doing so three times. Naomi argued that Ruth had been a good daughter-in-law but should now try to establish a new life for herself and even remarry. Thus, a passage that was clearly limited to a conversation between a bereaved woman and her daughter-in-law during a distraught period for both of them became artificially elevated into a template for dealing with applicants for conversion. It did not matter this this was centuries ago and in very different circumstances. The Orthodox rules therefore entailed not only turning prospective converts down, but also rejecting them twice more if they re-applied. And even after that, only considering them in the unlikely event that they still persisted. The clear hope was that the 'you-are-not-wanted' message would ensure people gave up and never even started the conversion process.

It might have been thought that this position would gradually soften as interfaith relations became much stronger, especially after the horrors of the Holocaust. Since then Jewish–Christian dialogue has leapt from being hardly existent to commonplace. However, as was discussed in Chapter 8, this period coincided with the rise in mixed-faith marriages. The Orthodox rabbinate was greatly opposed to such unions, and saw attempts by the non-Jewish partners of Jews to convert as being 'a backdoor to intermarriage'. Requests for conversion for the sake of the 'marriage motive' – as it was labelled – were seen as automatic proof of insincerity and grounds for rejection.

The opposition to conversion was not just a rabbinic matter, but was to be found amongst sections of the Jewish community at large. They felt that converts were 'different' or 'outsiders' who could never be fully integrated into Jewish life. Gabrielle spoke for many when she said:

> However sincere they are, they can never be one of us. Either you are born a Jew or you're not. It's in your genes and converts simply don't have them. It's either in your bloodline or it isn't.

This is a fascinating, though problematic, inversion of the *limpieza de sangre* (purity of blood) philosophy of the Spanish after the expulsion of the Jews in 1492. This resulted in several thousand Jews preferring to undertake an insincere conversion to Christianity in order to remain in the country, becoming known as Marranos or Conversos. The 'real' Christians could not reject the Conversos on religious grounds, being officially fellow Christians, and so insisted on proof of lineage before a marriage took place. In that way they ensured they were not aligning themselves with former Jews. Of course, all that occurred over five hundred years ago. Today, the rejection of converts by born-Jews is even more distasteful as it is not that far removed from concepts of Aryan purity and could be labelled Jewish racism. It is hardly a stance of which to be proud.

Examining the resistance

One reason for the antipathy of some Jews to converts is that they invariably have greater Jewish knowledge than many born Jews. They have studied Judaism in adulthood, rather than learnt it in childhood, and often have a much more sophisticated and informed understanding of it. The result is to make some born-Jews feel embarrassed at their comparative ignorance. In addition, the converts can also show greater commitment to the faith, having deliberately chosen it, rather than having been accidentally born into it. In many a synagogue, for instance, converts form a disproportionately high percentage of Religion School teachers. They are enthused enough to get out of bed early on a Sunday morning to teach the children, while born-Jews sleep on. This can be both admired and resented, making born-Jews feel they are being sidelined.

None of these reasons should have any place in modern Judaism. On the contrary, conversion should be restored to being as open and uncomplicated as it was in biblical times, when the desire to marry someone Jewish could mean adopting the Jewish faith too, if the person so wished. Marriage by itself cannot mean automatic conversion, but it should hold the prospect of a gateway, not a locked door. It is not just a matter of procedure, but of attitude: the request to convert should be seen as a compliment. In an age where there are many people without any religious affiliation at all, and there is no need to belong to a faith or else risk being cast adrift socially and economically, applications should be a source of pleasure rather than suspicion.

Given the ethical obligations and ritual demands of Judaism, it is ludicrous to wonder whether applicants are insincere. Even if they do not keep every single one of the traditions, they would be acting no differently from born-Jews. The latter are notorious for their pick-and-mix approach, keeping one custom but not another, yet never doubting that they feel at home in Judaism and identify as Jewish. It is why Karen was puzzled that her Jewish fiancé happily ate pork in restaurants, but was aghast at the thought of having it at home. As she explained:

> It seemed so illogical to me. I reckoned that you either kept *kosher* or you did not, whereas he saw the divide as being inside or outside the home. I still think one should be consistent, but I have come to realise that he thinks he *is* being consistent.

This is not to argue for abandoning standards, but it is to repudiate the notion that converts have to be holier than born-Jews to be accepted. The desire to join a Jewish family and keep a Jewish lifestyle should be sufficient.

This could also apply to those who wish to convert but who are not sure if they believe in God. It might seem strange that a person wants to adopt a faith without having faith, and to some it might sound outrageous. However, it reflects the fact that many partners of Jews admire the ethics of Judaism, the family life, the domestic rituals and the cycle of festivals. These are the features that attract them, even though they have no sense of a deity, nor any belief in a personal God. They may be disbelievers, but they are genuine in their desire to become Jewish and should be accepted. If there is a problem, it is more that we are locked into the word 'conversion', which implies having a faith, whereas they can be more accurately described as wanting to be naturalised. Like Ruth, quoted above as declaring that 'your people shall be my people', what they really want is to join the Jewish community. It is up to the community to accept that they may not be regular synagogue-goers, but they will be good Jewish atheists or agnostics, like so many born-Jews.

The benefits

If a greater degree of acceptance makes life easier for converts, it is also in the interest of Judaism itself. This can be seen in three separate ways. First, in terms of numbers. After the reign of King Solomon, Israel was divided into two kingdoms: the Southern Kingdom, consisting of two tribes loyal to his heirs, and the Northern Kingdom consisting of ten tribes. In 722 BCE, the Assyrian Empire conquered the Northern Kingdom, transported the ten tribes into different parts of the empire, into whose midst they disappeared and became known as the Ten Lost Tribes. It means that from then onwards, the Jewish population has only been two-twelfths of what it could have been. In addition, the period 1939–1945 saw a third of that remnant murdered by the Nazis. As was pointed out in Chapter 6, today's Jewry is therefore one-ninth of its possible size. When one adds the modern losses through assimilation, and subsequent worries over vanishing communities, then there is every reason to welcome the addition of converts. Numbers matter.

Whereas most other major world faiths do not worry whether they will continue or not, Jewish survival is a constant theme for both rabbinic sermons and Jewish sociologists, as it cannot be guaranteed on current figures. This certainly applies to British Jewry (see Chapter 1), which has seen a downward spiral for almost all of the past seven decades.

The second benefit arising from converts is, in the words of Rabbi Lionel Blue: 'They bring a "breath of fresh air" with them. In a declining population, genetic variation is much needed, lest it results in accidental inbreeding that borders on the incestuous.' Still, Rabbi Blue meant it more in a spiritual sense: that converts brought different perceptions and experiences which Judaism needed to take into account and absorb in order to stay relevant and fit for purpose. Although the congregation has heard sermons about social action for years, it was actually one of the converts who suggested setting up lunches for the homeless and made it happen, while another initiated communal fund-raising efforts for Bosnian Muslims refugees during the civil war in former Yugoslavia. They both had a wider perspective of the needs of others than we should have had, but lacked.

The third benefit is the effect that the conversion process has on the Jewish partners. In some, or perhaps in many cases, the Jewish partner has lapsed in their observances, or is inactive in synagogue life. Having a partner who wishes to convert forces them to reassess their own Jewish identity and what is important about it for them. It certainly means increasing their personal Jewish involvement, both to show their partner the full range of Jewish life and to assist them as they immerse themselves in it. This also entails attending the conversion course, ostensibly to be supportive, but in reality to upgrade their own Jewish knowledge.

For many born-Jews, their formal Jewish education had ceased around the age of *bar/bat mitzvah*, whereas now they are forced to re-engage at a much more mature and sophisticated level. This often leads to them taking on a leadership role within their local synagogue, be it organising events or sitting on committees. The result is that not only does the convert become Jewish, but the born-Jew becomes more Jewish and is transformed from a passive to an active member of the community

Who converts?

Those seeking to convert tend to fall into two broad categories, albeit with several subdivisions. The first are those who have a Jewish partner. In many instances, it is the first time they have had contact with Judaism. As Cathy described:

> All I knew about Jews was from a few RE lessons at school.
> I don't think I'd ever met a real Jew until I met Elliot, and
> by then I was 27.

Approximately half of those with a Jewish partner who
convert do so before marriage, albeit for a mixture of
motives. For some, it is in order to have 'the full works
and a white wedding in synagogue'; for others, it is 'I knew
it would please him, and also make life much easier for
his family'; for others still, it is because 'part of uniting
our lives is sharing a lifestyle, so I wanted to do that right
from the word go'. It is noticeable that these are largely
practical reasons, rather than spiritual ones, but they can
still be meaningful within the new partnership and new
household that is being created.

In addition, the conversion course is only undertaken
– and passed – by those who are prepared to devote time
to it and can demonstrate that it resonates with them. This
permissive attitude will certainly be deemed unacceptable
by the Orthodox, but it ignores two critical aspects. First,
if such converts are turned away, then it does not mean
they will separate, just that the Jewish person definitely
has no Jewish spouse and there is no Jewish household.
Second, as Judaism is a way of life, there is every possibility
that the convert's involvement will grow as the years pass
and as they feel more at home in Jewish family life. Of
course, there are also those marrying a Jew who do rejoice
in the faith aspect. As Greg explained:

> I never had a strong faith of my own, but I really feel
> at home in Judaism, so it felt right to adopt it before we
> got wed.

For others, however, conversion only comes after marriage and a process of slowly realising that one had been becoming Jewish without recognising it, and then deciding to formally take it on. For Marissa:

> Obviously, I knew Gary was Jewish before we married, but that had nothing to do with our relationship. He also played rugby, but that didn't make me want to take it up! It was only after we'd been married for some time and I'd accidentally led a Jewish life – through him not wanting pork at home, or him doing some of the domestic rituals with the children, such as Friday night candles – that I realised I rather liked it and had begun to see it as my tradition too.

The advent of children also led many to convert, as happened with Tanya:

> Religion didn't seem to matter so much when it was just the two of us. Either it didn't happen, or he sometimes went off to synagogue to do his own thing. But with the arrival of the kids, that changed everything. It was very important for us to be a united family. So, I contacted the rabbi and started the process.

In fact, Tanya's journey was in two parts, for her husband belonged to an Orthodox synagogue:

> His rabbi demanded that we move within walking distance to the synagogue, and both came to services regularly. Gavin was told that he could no longer attend football matches on Saturday afternoons. I went home

after that interview and burst into tears as it seemed that we would have to completely change our lifestyle and to a degree that neither of us felt comfortable with. It took a while to realise that I wanted a cat but had been offered a dog, and it was a version of Judaism that was not for us. So, I approached the local Reform rabbi and found that, although there were still expectations as to our commitment, it was much more in keeping with who we were. So now we do go to synagogue regularly, but have the same home and Gavin still gets to his football matches afterwards!

For some, Tanya's story is about an abysmal lowering of standards; for others, it is a victory for religious common sense.

In all these differently motivated scenarios, there is one common factor: that those converting tend to be disproportionately female rather than male, with a ratio of five to one. This is for two reasons. First, as has been discussed earlier, because of the traditional definition of Jewish status as a Jew being someone born of a Jewish mother (see Chapter 5). Thus, for a mixed-faith couple concerned about their children being recognised as Jewish, it has been imperative for the mother to convert if she was the non-Jewish partner; conversely, if the father was the non-Jewish partner, it did not have any impact on the child's status and so there was less incentive for him to convert.

Second, the obligation for males to undergo circumcision as part of the conversion process has been a major disincentive for men who were initially amenable to converting when marrying into a Jewish family, but baulked at the mention of such an operation. The custom goes back to the first book of the Bible and to the very first Jew, Abraham. Orthodox authorities will exempt someone from circumcision if there is medical evidence that it could be a threat to their health, as might be the case for a haemophiliac. However, such situations are rare, and the most common reasons for not wanting circumcision are the fear of the operation, worries about sexual performance afterwards or the act of changing one's body shape. These are all needless concerns, as there are no negative consequences of adult circumcision. But Reform rabbis recognise that they are still very powerful psychological barriers and can act as a deterrent. It has therefore been decided that circumcision is always regarded as the best option, but rather than lose those who might otherwise convert to Judaism, it is not necessary in cases where it can cause distress.

The second category of those converting is those who have no Jewish partner, known as *lishma* – those doing it for its own sake and without any emotional involvement. There are many rabbis who feel that this is by far the greatest test of sincerity and that the absence of 'the marriage motive' indicates a higher level of commitment. It is seen, therefore, as a purer route to Judaism. That description, though, reveals a certain bias, as everyone adopting Judaism has a motive: whether it be falling in love with someone Jewish or feeling more fulfilled personally within Judaism. There is self-interest in both scenarios. It is also irrelevant how one comes into contact with Judaism – through a Jewish partner, by reading a book on Jewish life, visiting a synagogue or having some other form of Jewish encounter. What matters is not the moment of introduction, but how one then reacts to it, and whether one feels it is something one wants to adopt.

Shirley, for instance, became interested in Judaism as a result of studying it at school for her GCSE course on Religious Education. When at university, she occasionally attended the Jewish Society. On graduating and settling in a new area, she visited the local synagogue, eventually asking to convert:

> I'm still in touch with most of my old schoolmates. Looking back, we all went through the same RE course, but I was the only one to decide that it meant something more. Now I'm Jewish and they are still what they always were. I guess something just clicked for me and from then on, I knew I'd be Jewish one day.

Similarly, there are a considerable number of non-Jews who marry someone Jewish each year, but only a small percentage who decide to also adopt Judaism.

The one caveat surrounding those converting 'for its own sake' is that they can lack the automatic support group that someone with a Jewish partner has immediately to hand. So much of Jewish life is home and family-based – what ingredients one can and cannot have when cooking, how to light the candles on a Friday night, what to do at Passover, how to put up a *mezuzah* – therefore, being part of a Jewish couple or extended family helps enormously. These and other rituals are all covered in the conversion course, but there is a big difference between learning about them and living them. Those who are alone in their path to Judaism have to find other ways of making them second nature. In fact, this is fast becoming an issue for synagogues to solve owing to a recent growth in conversions by those who are married to someone non-Jewish. This would not be possible via the Orthodox, for it would mean *creating* a mixed-faith marriage and, to their minds, turning a single-faith household into a confused one.

Reform rabbis were initially reluctant to countenance such applicants for the same reason, but became persuaded by cases such as that of Stephanie:

> I have always been religious, but also never felt entirely comfortable in church services. It was only in later life that I encountered Judaism and realised that it answered my spiritual needs. I am married to Terry, who is agnostic but has always been happy for me to pursue my religious interests, providing that they do not interfere with his life or upset our relationship.

As Terry explains:

> The way I see it is that Stephanie has her hobby – Judaism – and I have mine – golf – and we both do our own thing on a Saturday morning and then meet back at home.

Stephanie's local Reform rabbi recognised that, on the one hand, it would be hard for her to create a Jewish home life with a partner who did not share it; but, on the other hand, there was no doubting her sincerity and he certainly did not want her to adopt Judaism at the cost of her marriage. In recent years, therefore, it has been commonplace to accept converts in this situation, and also to recognise the reality that the balance of their Jewish life will shift from taking place both in the home and at the synagogue, to being primarily via the latter.

A variation of the *lishma* cases are rare but periodic instances when both partners in a non-Jewish couple each decide to become Jewish. Derek and Doris, for instance, had often discussed how they admired Jewish history or Jewish values, and one day looked at each other and said 'Why don't we think of becoming Jewish?' and jointly proceeded. In other cases, each partner had been thinking independently about Judaism, but had been nervous of possibly causing problems by telling the other, only to be delighted when it emerged that they were both thinking along the same lines, as Derek explains:

> In raising the subject, I was almost as nervous as when I proposed to her. I know that sounds daft, but being Jewish was really important to me, but I was also desperate not to say anything that would upset her. So, when she smiled and said she felt the same, it was just wonderful.

Another person with an equally happy story is Louise:

> When I met Roger, I explained that I was going to convert and had wanted to do so since I was a child. Roger wasn't Jewish, but this didn't put him off. In fact, he used to drive me to my classes and came to various events. On occasions, members of the congregation would comment on what a nice Jewish boy he was! We then became engaged and Roger said he would like to attend the classes, so that he knew about the religion and could support me and any children we had. When I contacted

our rabbi, she said that this was totally unacceptable and that as far as she was concerned, I was off the course, as I could not convert and then 'marry out'. I was devastated, hurt and cross.

After some time, I noticed in the *Jewish Chronicle* that there was a course entitled 'I'm Jewish my Partner Isn't'. Roger and I attended, and we were referred to the new rabbi who had started at the synagogue where I had been converting. This was the beginning of an amazing journey. I completed my conversion and Roger decided that Judaism answered a lot of questions that had turned him away from Christianity, so he then attended the conversion course.

We have now been members for twenty-eight years and the whole community have been our family and supported us throughout our Jewish life from birth, marriage and bereavement to sickness and health. We like to refer to our family as the 'thirteenth tribe' because our children have two parents who have converted, so the four of us have joined the twelve tribes of Israel and started something new, along with all the other double convert Jewish families out there.

Such cases are unusual, but are a powerful reminder that amid all the rabbinic rules and general statistics, there are warm hearts beating with trepidation at the personal journey that they are undertaking.

The conversion process

Whatever the motive and circumstances for conversion, the course is similar: it lasts at least a year, so as to experience the cycle of festivals, it covers knowledge of Jewish rituals, values, history, sacred texts and beliefs, and it involves participating in communal life as well as observing home ceremonies. The decision to accept a candidate onto the conversion course lies with the rabbi of each synagogue, and can lead to varying practices. Much depends on how much the person knows about Judaism and the rabbi's assessment of them. Some rabbis will insist that the person goes away to read more about the faith; others will ask them to attend services for a while, so as to see Judaism as it is, rather than their idea of it, which may be different; others will suggest they start lessons immediately, so as to get to grips with the reality and see if it is for them or not. It is at this initial stage that those who had approached the rabbi on a whim tend to drop out, realising that being Jewish is probably not really for them, whereas those who are committed proceed with the course.

It is a sign of the growing confidence of the Reform rabbinate in the value of what they are offering that they have just undertaken a radical new departure from previous rules. Until 2018, it was taken for granted that a person could only become Jewish if they were part of a synagogue, attended its conversion course and could experience local Jewish life. However, synagogues are only in a limited number of areas in the country and requests for conversion are increasingly coming from towns and villages where there is no Jewish community. This is either because changing demographic trends have meant that Jews are more widely dispersed, including those who have a non-Jewish partner wishing to convert. Alternatively, as was seen above, individuals without any family connections with Judaism and who have lived for many years in 'non-Jewish areas' are now applying. In response to this trend, an online course has been developed, led by a Reform rabbi, which allows the conversion to be undertaken through distance learning.

Those 'logging on' each week for services and for the classes may live hundreds of miles from each other, but find a rapport with the rabbi and camaraderie with each other. Applicants are also asked to travel to the nearest synagogue once a month so as to have 'hands-on' contact with communal life on the Sabbath, as well as participating in festivals. 'Online Judaism' may not be ideal, but it is highly significant, both as a recognition of changing lifestyles and as a willingness to respond positively to them.

At the end of the course, it is up to the rabbi to refer the candidate to the centralised examining board, the *Beit Din*, which interviews them and makes a final decision. It judges cases according to the candidate's knowledge and sincerity, recognising that not everyone is academic and that religious feelings can be expressed in different ways. To its great credit, the *Beit Din* is as much concerned with whether Judaism is right for the person converting, as it is with whether the person is right for Judaism. While the *Beit Din* is keen to ensure that converts will be a worthy addition to the faith, it also wants to prevent individuals being pressurised to convert by partners or in-laws. Immediately after the *Beit Din* session, the person goes to the *mikveh*, the ritual bath, and immerses themselves in its waters. It is a symbolic act, a whole-body experience coming after over a year of largely cerebral activity – thinking and studying – indicating the formal transition to a new religious identity.

At each of the *Beit Din's* monthly sittings, some ten people become Jewish. At one level, it can be seen as a succession of individual stories; on another level, it is the slow but steady heartbeat of the new trend of conversion to Judaism that has re-ignited after almost seventeen hundred years since Constantine banned it.

In many ways, the work of the *Beit Din* is the jewel in the Reform crown and should be celebrated much more. The legacy of the reservations of past generations towards conversion still seems to haunt current attitudes. It is noticeable, for instance, that synagogue newsletters advertise a host of congregational activities – from services to quiz nights to youth clubs – but rarely publicise their conversion course. They exist, but are still under the radar and only for those who request access, rather than being presented as one of many opportunities available as a normative part of communal life. It is time that Reform synagogues were not only much more proactive in offering conversion, but were proud of what they offer. A new balance needs to be struck – not being abrasive, yet stating loud and clear: 'If you are happy as you are, be it in another faith or no faith, that's fine; but those who want to join us are welcome and will be welcomed.'

12

The Way Forward...
and Will It Work?

As for what happens next...

No one doubts that British Jewry is entering a critical phase in its existence. Many of the certainties that sustained the community in the past have either disappeared or become frayed. The ultra-Orthodox may be growing, but only at the cost of living in a self-imposed ghetto – physically and mentally. It is a way of life that does not resonate with mainstream Jews. Meanwhile, many of British Jewry's now adult children are moving out of traditional areas. Some are intermarrying, or are marrying within the faith but having low birth rates, and some are no longer automatically affiliating to synagogues. It may be true that many are still engaged in Jewish cultural activities, via communal centres such as JW3 in London or through specialist groups such as the Jewish Music Institute, but that cultural affiliation is not necessarily being passed on to the next generation. For many of them, Judaism has changed from being their core identity to being their hobby, and like most people's hobbies, it is not necessarily shared by their children.

It should be noted that worrying about the future is part of the Jewish DNA. There is a romantic temptation for each generation to see itself as the last bastion, the final guardian of the eternal flame that is in danger of being extinguished. Back in the thirteenth century, a rabbi wrote to another in France: 'You and I are the last two Jews left, and we must strive to keep alive the faith our forefathers, lest it perish forever.' Several centuries later, his words may look like ridiculous hyperbole, but it was no doubt genuinely felt at the time. It is a caution that applies to today's situation too.

Rather than claiming that British Jewry is heading for an abyss – as some of the more hysterical commentators assert – it would be wiser to suggest that it is at a cross-roads. In many ways, it is epitomised by Dave and Jilly, who are Jewish parents with a puzzle:

> We brought up our three children in the same way in a nominally Orthodox home, mixing secular education with Jewish identity, being part of everyday life as well as members of our local synagogue. But to our surprise, the three have developed in radically different directions in terms of their religious life – with one becoming ultra-Orthodox, another rejecting Judaism entirely and our third child opting for Reform Judaism. The split between the children – now all in their 30s – is so extreme that both of us find it hard to relate to two of them any more, while it has also divided the siblings from each other.

It is fairly unusual for such a dramatic scenario to occur within the same family, but it reflects with uncanny precision the three diverse directions in which Jewish millennials in Britain are going.

Dave and Jilly's eldest child is Robert, who has now changed his name to the more biblical Reuven:

> He began to become more religious after going to university. He felt uncomfortable being away from home for the first time and floating around anonymously within a massive student population. He sought out the Jewish Society and met a charismatic chaplain from a group of self-styled Jewish missionaries who try to persuade lapsed or middle-of-the-road Jews to become more observant.

These Jewish 'missionaries' are not dangerous or financially manipulative, but they do have an agenda to change fellow Jews, especially those they sense are rudderless. They offer free meals, interesting talks, subsidised trips abroad and love-bomb those who attend. They are the Jewish equivalent of the Alpha programme, and while many young Jews enjoy their activities, without changing their lifestyle, others like Robert become *baal teshuvah*, or 'born again', and become Orthodox.

The result is that the people these programmes attract then only move within those circles. Robert/Reuven married an Orthodox girl, only eats *kosher* food, moved to a Jewish area of Manchester and will not travel on the Sabbath. Some would regard these as sacrifices; he sees them as his anchor. It also means he rarely sees his parents, and even when he does visit, he brings his own food.

The impact on the next generation is even more extreme, for he is reluctant for his children to be in a home where religious standards are, in his mind, lax. Meanwhile, his parents admire his commitment to Judaism but regret the fact that they have little in common with him and are walking a tightrope to retain a relationship with their grandchildren.

Their daughter Anna, by contrast, has chosen to marry someone non-Jewish. She is typical of the one in three British Jews who fall in love across the religious divide. Anna and her non-Jewish husband decided to save domestic rows and fights over the children by making their home a religion-free zone. She does not mind doing 'Jewish stuff' elsewhere, and so the children have an inkling of their Jewish heritage through home ceremonies at her parents or occasional visits to synagogue on the festivals. She finds Robert/Reuven almost impossible to have a relationship with, as his Judaism dominates all aspects of his life, whereas hers is just a detail, alongside her work, book club and running group. Dave and Jilly were deeply upset:

> We were devastated when Anna announced she was marrying out of the faith, for although we like her partner, we saw it as an indictment of her upbringing and worried that it might threaten Jewish continuity. However, to our surprise, we find it much easier to get along with Anna and her non-Jewish husband than with Robert/Reuven and his Orthodox family. Despite the faith divide, they share the same values and everyday experiences as us.

The youngest, Jeremy, has chosen a third path. He wanted to find a way of marrying tradition with modernity and so joined a Reform synagogue, which seeks to adapt Judaism to changing conditions:

> I wanted a synagogue where women are considered fully equal and not only sit together with the men (unlike the Orthodox) but can lead services and be rabbis.

For Jeremy, and many young Jews like him, values such as equality and inclusivity are vital, which also applies to divorcees, single parents, couples living together and LGBT+ inclusion. Jeremy cannot understand why his father and mother still belong to an Orthodox synagogue, even though they think and practise Reform. His parents justify themselves by responding:

> We agree that his form of Judaism is more principle-led than ours, but feel reluctant to switch from the synagogue we've always known. It feels comfortable, even if we barely attend more than twice a year.

Looking at the larger picture, the family exemplifies how British Jewry is becoming increasingly polarised, with the common factor of millennials rejecting their parents' Judaism, but doing so in different ways. The big question mark is which of these trends will become the dominant one – becoming more Orthodox, more secular or trying to balance Jewish identity with a modern lifestyle?

When one is standing at a crossroads, what usually determines which route one takes is the signposting, and whether it is clear and helpful.

This book has highlighted a massive own-goal: we have spent so many years arguing about who can and cannot come through the front door, that we have taken our eyes off the backdoor, and the next generation is running away. If we are lucky, they will get halfway down the garden and turn back because they miss home. But if they find a more compelling alternative, they will climb over the wall and never come back – and we will all share some of the responsibility. In the words of the prophet Ezekiel (34:4–5):

> You have not brought back those who have strayed, or looked for the lost; but have driven them away through an uncompromising approach and they have been scattered for want of anyone to care for them.

Yet, here is the good news – Reform has stopped obsessing at the front door, and this book traces the remarkable attempt to step back, reassess the structure of the whole house, see how inhabitable it is and implement what needs to change.

All this means that rabbis need to both provide a caring home for those seeking religious security, as well as a flexible Judaism for those who want to extend the borders, or weave in and out. In the age of the millennials, Jewish geography has become more complex, but full of opportunities.

Still, the question remains: will it work? Jewish history suggests that the answer is 'yes'. The Jewish story is an amazing rollercoaster of high and lows, with Golden Ages, alternating with periods of persecution, while eras of antisemitism have interchanged with times of integration. Throughout it all, individual families may have been lost, but the community at large has continued.

It is the main thesis of this book, though, that when Jews are in control of their own destiny, some paths are better than others. Emigration to Israel may bring personal fulfilment for some, but we see a bright future for British Jewry. It was no accident that the first Reform synagogue to be formed, back in 1840, decided that its name would be 'The West London Synagogue of British Jews', which was partly an advertisement of its location, but also a strong message about its identity – Jewish *and* British.

Another 'solution' – retreating into an insular world of Orthodoxy that eschews contact with wider society – may be seen as God's will by some, but is not our understanding of what being Jewish means. It may take effort to be part of both worlds, but we belong to both and have to navigate the challenges that dual citizenship entails. It is also necessary to resist the temptation to hold on to the status quo, which can be a much more comfortable place to reside, but carries the danger of creating modern orthodoxies that impede progress.

That is why it has been entirely appropriate to embrace dramatic changes that have transformed the Jewish land-scape, whether it be female rabbis, mixed-faith marriages, transliterated Hebrew or marrying same-sex couples. Each may, at first, have been treated with nervousness and reluctance, but we have been courageous enough to overcome both the naysayers who predicted that Judaism would collapse and our own inclination to opt for pottering along without upsetting any religious apple-carts. For if rules have been in the way of progress, or have been laden with unethical assumptions, then they needed to be bypassed, if not overturned.

Camilla's story epitomises the stark choice to be taken when such forks in the road appear, especially when legal niceties threaten to harm real individuals:

I came from a traditional Jewish family in Liverpool and always envisaged getting married and having children. Unfortunately, that longed-for husband never appeared. After much soul-searching as to my priorities and values, as well as a lot of research, at the age of 43 I decided to become a single parent and underwent fertility treatment. It became apparent that I would not only need donor sperm, but also a donor egg. With no Jewish egg donors available, I opted for a non-Jewish egg donor, realising that this might raise complications as to the status of any child. It proved successful, as did the pregnancy.

After the birth, I sought to clarify the baby boy's status. When I approached an Orthodox rabbi, I was told that because the genetic material – the egg – was not from a Jewish woman, then despite me being Jewish and bringing up my son as Jewish in a Jewish home, he would not be Jewish. The only way he could be Jewish was if he underwent a process of conversion that would take around eighteen months. It was heart-breaking.

However, when I approached a Reform rabbi, I was informed that as I was the birth mother and legal mother, then my son could be considered Jewish. All that was required was to have a short ceremony officially welcoming him into the world and into the Jewish religion.

To be fair to the Orthodox rabbi, he admitted that it was a grey area and open to interpretation. But he still took the maximalist view and demanded that Camilla jump through another hurdle, despite the many she had already endured. The Reform rabbi also recognised it was a grey area, but sought to make it as simple as possible. As another Reform rabbi, Jason Holtz, not involved in that case, once put it:

Judaism isn't the National Trust – trying so hard to preserve the past of a house that can no longer be lived in and whose furniture has signs saying: 'Keep off!'. Rather, it is the deepest creative expression of Jews, inspired by our religious inheritance, but not limited to preserving its current form.[1]

It is unwise to predict the future, but we can be certain about the present, especially if we want to try to shape that future, even if other factors may have their influence too. British Jewry needs to hear less of 'Thou shalt' and more of 'These are the options you have'.

Tradition is about the past, and though it may command respect, it should not be the automatic rulebook for the present. The Orthodox authorities will, of course, oppose any accommodation with modern trends, and there may be some within Reform circles who feel the same. It is vital, though, that we acknowledge them too and find ways of extending the Jewish umbrella to those Jews who are part of their congregations, as well as all those who feel excluded from them. To misquote Michael Jackson:

It don't matter if you're male or female
straight or gay
married or not
with a Jew or a non-Jew
a believer or not sure
kosher or Jewish-style.
It's a turf war on a global scale.
I'd rather hear both sides of the tale.

---

1   *Highlight*, Bromley Reform Synagogue newsletter, May 2018, p.4.

And we need not only to hear, but also to respond positively with the words – 'Please come in, because you are welcome here!'

Glossary of Hebrew words

Acher, other

Achi, my brother

Agunah (pl. *agunot*), a woman still 'chained' to her ex-husband

Amidah, central prayer of the Jewish liturgy

Anusim, Jews forced to abandon Judaism

B'rit ahavah, covenant of love

B'rit ahuvim, lovers' covenant

B'rit, covenant

Baal teshuvah, 'born again'

Bar/bat mitzvah, coming-of-age ceremony

Beit Din, rabbinic court

Cohen (pl. *cohanim*), Jewish priest

Halakhah, Jewish law

Hanukkiah, nine-branched candelabrum

Havdalah, religious ceremony marking the end of the Sabbath

Heder, Sunday school

Huppah, canopy used in the Jewish wedding service

Kaddish, memorial prayer for the dead

Kashrut, Jewish dietary laws

Ketubbah, marriage document

Kiddush, refreshments after a religious service

Kiddushin, holiness

Kippah, ritual head covering

Kol Nidrei, holiest night of the Jewish year

Kosher, conforming to Jewish dietary laws

Lishma, those converting to Judaism for its own sake

Mamzer, illegitimate child

Mezuzah, scroll with religious text for attaching to a doorpost

Mikveh, ritual bath

Minyan, quorum of ten adults required for some sections of religious services

Mitzvah, command, also good deed

Rabba, title for Orthodox women who are ordained

Rosh Hashanah, Jewish New Year

Rosh Hodesh, first day of the Hebrew month, also an occasion when many women's groups now meet

Seder, ritual feast at the start of Passover

Shabbat, the Sabbath – Judaism's day of rest

Shekhinah, the presence (of God), also representing female attributes of God

Shema, prayer recited at morning and evening services

Shivah, the first week of mourning after the loss of a close relative

Simhat bat, welcome ceremony for newborn daughters

Tallit, prayer shawl

Tikkun olam, repairing a fragmented world

To'evah, abomination

Torah, the Five Books of Moses – the first five books of the Bible